Mitchell Educational Series

Auto Body Repair

Student Technician's Manual

Robert Scharff
James E. Duffy
Michael Crandell

Mitchell International

Mitchell International

NOTICE TO THE READER

Publisher does not warrant or guarantee any of the products described herein or perform any independent analysis in connection with any of the product information contained herein. Publisher does not assume, and expressly disclaims, any obligation to obtain and include information other than that provided to it by the manufacturer.

The reader is expressly warned to consider and adopt all safety precautions that might be indicated by the activities herein and to avoid all potential hazards. By following the instructions contained herein, the reader willingly assumes all risks in connection with such instructions.

The publisher makes no representation or warranties of any kind, including but no limited to, the warranties of fitness for particular purpose or merchantability, nor are any such representations implied with respect to the material set forth herein, and the publisher takes no responsibility with respect to such material. The publisher shall not be liable for any special, consequential, or exemplary damages resulting, in whole or part, from the readers' use of, or reliance upon, this material.

EDITORIAL COUNCIL

Vice President, Database Strategy & Licensing Steve Hansen
Vice President, Database Communications & Development Tom Fleming
Director, Parts Database, Data Acquisition Ernie Tate ❚ **Director, Editorial Operations** Pat Rice
Manager, Collision Repair Gilbert Silva
Manager, Electronic Product Database Development Greg McDowell

PRODUCT MANAGEMENT/ADMINISTRATIVE SUPPORT

Vice President and General Manager, Publications Marc Brungger
Circulation Director Cheryl Witt ❚ **Senior Product Manager** Liz Goldberg
Project Management Sheila White/Jeff Pirino ❚ **Graphic Design** Larry Barnett/Jennifer Therieau
Product Support *Senior Specialist* Lorraine Macuse ❚ *Specialist* John Sulio
Administrative Services Susan Grimes ❚ **Product Coordination** Pam Halstead
Technical Library Charlotte Norris/Deborah Hickman

CUSTOMER SERVICE NUMBERS

Subscription/Billing Information **1-800-238-9111** • **619-578-6550 Ext. 8508** • **Fax 619-566-3345**
Product Information **1-800-854-7030** • **619-576-6550 Ext. 8220** • **Fax 1-888-256-7969/619-549-0629**
Or Write **P.O. Box 26260** • **San Diego, CA 92196-0260**

MITCHELL INTERNATIONAL
9889 Willow Creek Road
P.O. Box 26260
San Diego, CA 92196-0260

1 2 3 4 5 6 7 8 9 10 XXX 02 01 00 99 98 97

ISBN 0-7668-0632-4
Library of Congress Catalog Card Number: 96-47077

Table of Contents

Figure Credits

Courtesy of Audi: Figure SA2-3 (3c)

Courtesy of Black and Decker, Inc.: Figure SA4-1 (s)

Courtesy of Blackhawk Automotive, Inc.: Figures SA 4-1 (u) and SA4-1 (v)

Courtesy of Chicago Pneumatic Tool Division: Figures SA4-1 (f), SA4-1 (g), and SA4-1 (k)

Courtesy of Chief Automotive Systems, Inc.: Figure SA4-1 (x)

Courtesy of Chrysler Corporation: Figure SA2-3 (3b)

Courtesy of Delta International Machinery Corp: Figure SA4-1 (p)

Courtesy of DuPont Automotive Products: Figures SA19-1 (1 through 3)

Courtesy of Florida Pneumatic Mfg.: Figures SA4-1 (d), SA4-1 (e), SA4-1 (i)

Courtesy of HAKO Minuteman, Inc.: Figure SA4-1 (r)

Courtesy of Mazda Motor of America: Figure SA2-3 (3a)

Courtesy of Mitchell International: All of the art shown in Shop Assignment 10-4

Courtesy of Moog Automotive Inc.: Figures SA2-3 (2a) and SA2-3 (2b)

Courtesy of PPG Refinishing Industries: Figures SA21-2 (1 through 9)

Courtesy of Rotary Lift Corp: Figure SA4-1 (w)

Courtesy of Sealed Power Corp: Figures SA2-3 (1a), SA2-3 (1b)

Courtesy of Snap-on-Tools Corporation: Figures SA4-1 (q), SA4-1 (t)

*SA denotes Shop Assignment

Chapter 1

Body/Paint Shop Work and Safety Procedures

Shop Assignment 1-1

Name_____ Date _____ Instructor Review _____

Shop Layout

1. Make a line drawing of your school's autobody shop area. In the drawing, indicate the location of the following:

   1. Fire extinguishers
   2. Lifts
   3. Spray booth
   4. Frame machine
   5. Metal work stalls
   6. Paint prep stalls
   7. Clean up stalls
   8. Air compressor
   9. Air transformers
   10. Tool storage
   11. Personal equipment storage
   12. Doors

   13. Emergency exits
   14. Vent fants
   15. Paint mixing area
   16. Paint storage area
   17. Hazardous waste disposal
   18. Paint gun cleaning area
   19. Work benches
   20. Emergency eyewash station
   21. Hand washing area
   22. Non-smoking area
   23. Vacuum system

2. Complete this chart for each fire extinguisher in the shop:

Type	Location	Fire Fuel	Contents	Color of Label

Shop Assignment 1-2

Name_____ Date _____ Instructor Review _____

Personal Safety Equipment and Procedures

1. The student will demonstrate to the instructor how to properly fit and wear the following safety equipment:

When Is This Worn?

A. **Eye Protection**
   Safety glasses _____
   Face shield _____

B. **Lung Protection**
   Dust mask _____
   Cartridge respirator _____
   Supplied air respirator _____

C. **Ear Protection**
   Ear plugs _____

D. **Hand Protection**
   Impervious gloves _____
   Work gloves _____

E. **Skin Protection**
   Paint suit _____

2. Explain how to properly lift a 75 lb. bumper assembly from the floor to a work bench. _____
   _____
   _____

3. What can happen if sanding, dust or paint fumes are not properly vented from the shop area?
   _____
   _____

Shop Assignment 1-3

Name_____ Date _____ Instructor Review _____

MSDS Sheets

Refer to the Material Safety Data Sheets on pages 6 through 8 to answer the following questions.

1. What should be used to put out a fire fueled by this material? _____
   _____

2. What is the specific effect of butylacetate? _____
   _____

3. What is the density of this vapor? _____
   _____

4. What are the hazardous decomposition products? _____
   _____

5. What should be done if this material is spilled? _____

   _____
   _____
   _____
   _____
   _____
   _____

MSDS NO. 19-3
CHROMABASE® BASEMAKERS

REFINISH SALES
January 1, 1995

MATERIAL SAFETY
DATA SHEET

CHROMABASE® BASEMAKERS

Section I - Manufacturer

Manufacturer:
    DuPont Co.
    Automotive
    Wilmington, Delaware 19898
Telephone:
    Product information (800)441-7515
    Medical emergency (800) 441-3637
    Transportation emergency (800) 424-9300 (CHEMTREC)
Product: Chromabase® Basemakers(S7160S, S7175S, S7185S,
  7105S, 7155S, 7160S, 7175S, 7185S, 7195S).
OSHA Hazard Class: Flammable liquid
DOT Shipping Name: Paint, UN1263
Hazardous Materials Information: See Section X.

Section II - Hazardous Ingredients (See Section X)

Ingredients	CAS No.	Vapor Pressure (20°C. mm Hg)	Exposure Limits *
1. Acetic anhydride	108-24-7 1.0	5 ppm-A,O Ceiling	
2. Acetone	67-64-1	184.0 750 ppm-A 1000 ppm-O 1000 ppm-A 15 min(STEL)	
3. Acrylic polymer	Not Available	None-None-A, O	
4. Aromatic hydrocarbon	64742-95-6	10.0 25 ppm-A,O as Trimethyl benzene	
5. Butyl acetate	123-86-4 8.0	150 ppm-A,O 200 ppm-A,O 15 min(STEL)	
6. Diisobutyl ketone	108-83-8 1.7	25 ppm-A 50 ppm-O	
7. Ethyl acetate	141-78-6 76.0	400 ppm-A,O	
8. Ethyl 3-ethoxy propionate	763-69-9 Unkn	None-A,O	
9. Ethylene glycol monobutyl ether acetate	112-07-2 0.3	20 ppm-D Skin None-A,O	
10. Hexyl acetate isomers	88230-35-7	0.7 50 ppm-A None-O	
11. Isopropyl alcohol	67-63-0 33.0	400 ppm-A,O 500 ppm-A 15 min(STEL)	
12. Ketone solvent	71808-49-6	5.8 None-A,O	
13. Medium mineral spirits	64742-88-7	Unkwn None-A,O 100 ppm-D	
14. Methyl amyl ketone	110-43-0 2.2	50 ppm-A 100 ppm-O	

15. Methyl ethyl ketone	78-93-3 71.0	200 ppm-A,O 300 ppm-A 15 min(STEL) 200 ppm-D 8&12 hr TWA	
16. Methyl isoamyl ketone	110-12-3 4.5	50 ppm-A None-O	
17. Methyl isobutyl ketone	108-10-1 15.0	50 ppm-A 100 ppm-O 75 ppm-A 15 min(STEL)	
18. n-Butyl alcohol	71-36-3 5.5	50 ppm-A C Skin 100 ppm-O 25 ppm-D 50 ppm-D 15 min TWA	
19. n-Pentyl propionate	624-54-4 1.2	None -A,O	
20. Primary amyl acetate	628-63-7 4.0	100 ppm-A.O	
21. Propionic acid, n-butyl ester	590-01-2 3.4	None-A,O	
22. Toluene	108-88-3 36.7	50 ppm-A Skin 200 ppm-O 300 ppm-O Ceiling 500 ppm- O 10 min MAX 50 ppm-D 8&12 hr TWA	
23. VM&P Naphtha	64742-89-8	Unkwn 300 ppm-A,O 400 ppm-O 15 min(STEL) 100 ppm-D	
24. Xylene	1330-20-7	25.0 100 ppm-A,O 150 ppm-A,O 15 min(STEL)	

A = ACGIH TLV; O= OSHA; D = DuPont internal limit; S=Supplier
  Furnished limit; STEL = Short Term Exposure Limit; Ceiling.

Section III - Physical Data

Evaporation rate: Less than ether
  Vapor Density: Heavier than air
  Solubility in water: Miscible
  Percent volatile by volume: 86.2% - 99.8%
  Percent volatile by weight: 81.4% - 99.8%
  Boiling range: 54°C- 221°C/129°F- 429°F
  Gallon weight: 6.61 - 7.40 lb/gallon

Section IV - Fire and Explosion Data

Flash point (closed cup): See Section X for exact values.
  Flammable limits: 0.8 -13.0%
  Extinguishing media: Water spray, foam, carbon dioxide, dry chemical.
  Special fire fighting procedures: Full protective equipment, including self-contained breathing apparatus, is recommended. Water from fog nozzles may be used to cool closed containers to prevent pressure build up.
  Unusual fire & explosion hazards: When heated above the flash point, emits flammable vapors which, when mixed with air, can burn or

be explosive. Fine mists or sprays may be flammable at temperatures below the flash point.

Section V - Health Hazard Data

General effects

Ingestion: Gastrointestinal distress. In the unlikely event of ingestion, call a physician immediately and have the names of ingredients available.

Inhalation: May cause nose and throat irritation. Repeated and prolonged overexposure to solvents may lead to permanent brain and nervous system damage. Eye watering, headaches, nausea, dizziness and loss of coordination are signs that solvent levels are too high. If affected by inhalation of vapor or spray mist, remove to fresh air. If breathing difficulty persists, or occurs later, consult a physician.

Skin or eye contact: May cause irritation or burning of the eyes. Repeated or prolonged liquid contact may cause skin irritation with discomfort and dermatitis. In case of eye contact, immediately flush with plenty of water for at least 15 minutes; call a physician. In case of skin contact, wash with soap and water. If irritation occurs, contact a physician.

Specific Effects:

Acetic anhydride - Contact may cause skin burns. Causes eye corrosion and permanent injury. May be a weak skin sensitizer. May cause temporary upper respiratory and/or lung irritation with cough, difficult breathing, or shortness of breath Inhalation overexposure may cause lung injury, fluid in the lung, and difficulty in breathing. Exposure to very high vapor concentrations may cause ulcerations of the nasal mucosa. Prolonged overexposure to the vapor may cause conjunctivitis and photophobia. **Aromatic hydrocarbon** - Laboratory studies with rats have shown that petroleum distillates cause kidney damage and kidney or liver tumors. These effects were not seen in similar studies with guinea pigs, dogs, or monkeys. Several studies evaluating petroleum workers have not shown a significant increase of kidney damage or an increase in kidney or liver tumors. May cause temporary upper respiratory and/or lung irritation with cough, difficult breathing, or shortness of breath. **Butyl acetate** - May cause abnormal liver function. Tests for embryotoxic activity in animals has been inconclusive. Has been toxic to the fetus in laboratory animals at doses that are toxic to the mother. **Diisobutyl ketone** - Extremely high oral and inhalation doses in laboratory animals have shown weight changes in various organs such as the liver, brain, heart, and adrenal gland. In addition liver and kidney injury were observed at the extremely high inhalation level. There was a slight depression in the white blood cell count. Repeated exposure may cause allergic skin rash, itching, swelling. **Ethyl acetate** - Prolonged and repeated high exposures of laboratory animals resulted in secondary anemia with and increase in white blood cells; fatty degeneration, cloudy swelling and excess of blood in various organs. **Ethyl 3-ethoxy propionate** - Has been toxic to the fetus in laboratory animals at dosed that are toxic to the mother. **Ethylene glycol monobutyl ether acetate:** Can be absorbed through the skin in harmful amounts. May destroy red blood cells. May cause abnormal kidney function. **Isopropyl alcohol** - Ingestion studies on laboratory animals showed that very high oral doses caused increased liver and kidney weights. **Ketone solvent** - Inhalation overexposure may cause lung injury, fluid in the lung, and difficulty in breathing. Ingestion studies on laboratory animals showed that very high oral doses caused increased liver and kidney weights. High doses in laboratory animals have shown nonspecific effects such as irritation, weight loss, moderate blood changes. **Mineral spirits, VM&P Naphtha** - Laboratory studies with rats have shown that petroleum distillates cause kidney damage and kidney or liver tumors. These effects were not seen in similar studies with guinea pigs, dogs, or monkeys. Several studies evaluating petroleum workers have not shown a significant increase of kidney damage or an

increase in kidney or liver tumors. May cause temporary upper respiratory and/or lung irritation with cough, difficult breathing, or shortness of breath. **Methyl amyl ketone** - Ingestion studies on laboratory animals showed that very oral doses caused increased liver and kidney weights. **Methyl ethyl ketone** - High concentration have caused embryotoxic effects in laboratory animals. Methyl ethyl ketone has been demonstrated to potentiate (i.e., shorten the time of onset) the peripheral neuropathy caused by either n-hexane or methyl n-butyl ketone. MEK by itself has not been demonstrated to cause peripheral neuropathy. Liquid splashes in the eye may result in chemical burns. **Methyl isoamyl ketone** - Extremely high oral doses in laboratory animals have shown weight changes in various organs such as the liver, kidney and adrenal gland. In addition, liver injury was observed. **Methyl isobutyl ketone** - Recurrent overexposure may result in liver and kidney injury. **n-Butyl alcohol** - Liquid splashes in the eye may result in chemical burns. May cause abnormal blood forming function with anemia. Recurrent overexposure may result in liver and kidney injury. Can be absorbed through the skin in harmful amounts. **n-Pentyl propionate** - Repeated or prolonged liquid contact may cause skin irritation with discomfort and dermatitis. May cause eye irritation with discomfort, tearing, or blurred vision. Material is irritating to mucous membranes and upper respiratory tract. **Primary amyl acetate** - Recurrent overexposure may result in liver and kidney injury. **Toluene** - Recurrent overexposure may result in liver and kidney injury. High airborne levels have produced irregular heart beats in animals and occasional palpitations in humans. Rats exposed to very high airborne levels have exhibited high frequency hearing deficits. The significance of this to man is unknown. **WARNING:** This chemical is known to the State of California to cause birth defects or other reproductive harm. **Xylene** - High concentration have caused embryotoxic effects in laboratory animals. Recurrent overexposure may result in liver and kidney injury. Can be absorbed through the skin in harmful amounts.

Section VI - Reactivity Data

Stability: Stable
  Incompatibility (materials to avoid): None reasonably foreseeable.
  Hazardous decomposition products: CO, CO_2, smoke.
  Hazardous polymerization: Will not occur.

Section VII - Spill or Leak Procedures

Steps to be taken in case material is released or spilled: Do not breathe vapors. Do not get in eyes or on skin. Wear a positive pressure supplied air vapor/particulate respirator (NIOSH/MSHA TC-19C), eye protection, gloves and protective material. Remove sources of ignition. Absorb with inert material. Ventilate area. Pour liquid decontaminate solution over the spill and allow to sit 10 minutes, minimum. Typical decontamination solutions are:

	20% Surfactant (Tergitol TMN 10)
	80% Water
or	0-10% Ammonia
	2-5% Detergent
	Balance water

Pressure can be generated. Do not seal container. After 48 hours, material may be sealed and disposed of.

Waste disposal method: Do not allow material to contaminate ground water systems. Incinerate absorbed material in accordance with federal, state, and local requirements. Do not incinerate in closed containers.

Section VIII - Special Protection Information

Respiratory: Do not breathe vapors or mists. Wear a positive pressure supplied air respirator (NIOSH/MSHA (TC-19C) while mixing activator with any paint or clear enamel, during application and until all vapors and spray mists are exhausted. Individuals with a history of lung or breathing problems or prior reaction to isocyanate should not use or be exposed to this product. Do not permit anyone without protection in the painting area. Follow the respirator manufacturer's directions for respirator use.

Ventilation: Provide sufficient ventilation in volume and pattern to keep contaminants below applicable OSHA requirements.

Protective clothing: Neoprene gloves and coveralls are recommended.

Eye protection: Desirable in all industrial situations. Include splash guards or side shields.

Section IX - Special Precautions

Precautions to be taken in handling and storing: Observe label precautions. Keep away from heat, sparks and flame. Close container after each use. Ground containers when pouring. Wash thoroughly after handling and before eating or smoking. Do not store above 120°F.

Other precautions: Do not sand, flame cut, braze or weld dry coating without a NIOSH/MSHA approved respirator or appropriate ventilation.

Section X - Other Information

Section 313 Supplier Notification: The chemicals listed below with percentages are subject to the reporting requirements of Section 313 of the Emergency Planning and Right-To-Know Act of 1986 and of 40 CFR 372.

PRODUCT CODE   **INGREDIENTS** (See Section II)

S-7160S   5, 8, 11, 14, 15(18%),22(9%), 23(35%), 24(6%), GAL WT: 6.61 WT PCT SOLIDS: 0.17 VOL PCT SOLIDS: 0.13 SOLVENT DENSITY: 6.61 VOC: 6.5 H: 2 F: 3 R: 0   FLASH PT: -73L OSHA STORAGE: IB

S-7175S   2(9%), 5, 11, 14, 17(5%), 21, 23, 24(7%), GAL WT: 6.64 WT PCT SOLIDS: 0.17 VOL PCT SOLIDS: 0.13 SOLVENT DENSITY: 6.64 VOC: 6.6 H: 2 F: 3 R: 0   FLASH PT: -73L OSHA STORAGE: IB

S-7185S   5, 6, 11, 13, 14, 15(9%), 21, 23, GAL WT: 6.68 WT PCT SOLIDS: 0.17 VOL PCT SOLIDS: 0.13 SOLVENT DENSITY: 6.68 VOC: 6.6 H: 2 F: 3 R: 0   FLASH PT: -73L OSHA STORAGE: IB

7105S   1, 3, 5, 23, GAL WT: 7.40 WT PCT SOLIDS: 18.60 VOL PCT SOLIDS: 13.72 SOLVENT DENSITY: 6.98 VOC: 6.0 H: 2 F: 3 R: 0 FLASH PT: -73L OSHA STORAGE: IB

7155S   2(58%), 10, 11, 20,22(13%), 23, GAL WT: 6.69 WT PCT SOLIDS: 0.17 VOL PCT SOLIDS: 0.13 SOLVENT DENSITY: 6.69 VOC: 6.6 H: 2 F: 3 R: 0   FLASH PT: -20L OSHA STORAGE: IB

7160S   5, 8, 11, 14, 15(18%),22(9%), 23, 24(6%), GAL WT: 6.61 WT PCT SOLIDS: 0.17 VOL PCT SOLIDS: 0.13 SOLVENT DENSITY: 6.61 VOC: 6.5 H: 2 F: 3 R: 0   FLASH PT: -73L OSHA STORAGE: IB

7175S   2(10%), 5, 7, 21,22(5%), 23, 24(28%), GAL WT: 7.09 WT PCT SOLIDS: 0.71 VOL PCT SOLIDS: 0.60 SOLVENT DENSITY: 7.08 VOC: 7.0 H: 2 F: 3 R: 0   FLASH PT: -73L OSHA STORAGE: IB

7185S   4, 6, 14, 17(4%), 18(8%), 19, 21, 23, GAL WT: 6.68 WT PCT SOLIDS: 0.17 VOL PCT SOLIDS: 0.13 SOLVENT DENSITY: 6.68 VOC: 6.6 H: 2 F: 3 R: 0   FLASH PT: -73L OSHA STORAGE: IB

7195S   6, 9(1%), 12, 16, 18(9%), 19, 23, GAL WT: 6.69 WT PCT SOLIDS: 0.18 VOL PCT SOLIDS: 0.14 SOLVENT DENSITY: 6.69 VOC: 6.6 H: 2 F: 3 R: 0   FLASH PT: -73L OSHA STORAGE: IB

Notice: The data in this material safety data sheet relate only to the specific material designated herein and do not relate to use in combination with any other material or in any process.

Product Manager - Refinish Sales

Rev. 1/95

Prepared by T.R. Louer,CIH
(302) 774-8303

Refer to the Material Safety Data Sheets on pages 10 through 12 to answer the following questions.

1. What safety equipment must be worn when using this paint? _____

   _____

2. What are the symptoms of overexposure? _____

   _____

3. What should you do if you splash the paint into your eye? _____

   _____

4. What can happen if you have repeated and prolonged overexposure to this paint? _____

   _____

5. Why is proper ventilation important? _____

   _____

MSDS NO. 17
URO® FINISHES

REFINISH SALES
January 1, 1995

MATERIAL SAFETY
DATA SHEET

URO® FINISHES

Section I - Manufacturer

Manufacturer:
DuPont Co.
Automotive
Wilmington, Delaware 19898

Telephone:
Product information (800)441-7515
Medical emergency (800) 441-3637
Transportation emergency (800) 424-9300 (CHEMTREC)

Product: URO® Products(1075S, 1080S, 1082S, 1085S, 1095S, 1120S, 11125S, 1130S, 1135S, 1140S, 1220S, 2080S, 2082S, 2085S)

OSHA Hazard Class: Flammable liquid

DOT Shipping Name: Paint Related Material, UN1263; Paint, UN1263

Hazardous Materials Information: See Section X.

Section II - Hazardous Ingredients (See Section X)

Ingredients	CAS No.	Vapor Pressure (20°C. mm Hg)	Exposure Limits *
1. Acrylic polymer A	70942-12-0	None	None-A,O
2. Acrylic polymer B	70942-12-0	None	None-A,O
3. Acrylic polymer C	80010-53-3	None	None-A,O
4. Acrylic polymer D	Not Available	None	None-A,O
5. Aliphatic polyisocyanate resin	28182-81-2	None	0.5 mg/m³-S 1 mg/m³-S 15 min(STEL) None-A,O
6. Aliphatic polymeric isocyanate	3779-63-3	None	0.5 mg/m³-S 1 mg/m³-S 15 min(STEL) None-A,O
7. Aromatic hydrocarbon A	64742-95-6	10.0	25 ppm-A,O as Trimethyl benzene
8. Aromatic hydrocarbon B	64742-94-5	10.0	100 ppm-D None-A,O
9. Barium sulfate	727-43-7	None	10 mg/m³-A 15 mg/m³-O 5 mg/m³-O Resp
10. Butyl acetate	123-86-4	8.0	150 ppm-A,O 200 ppm-A,O 15 min(STEL)
11. Calcium carbonate	471-34-1	None	10 mg/m³-A 15 mg/m³-O 5 mg/m³-O Resp
12. Diatomaceous Earth	7631-86-9	None	10 mg/m³-A None-O
13. Ethyl acetate	141-78-6	76.0	400 ppm-A,O
14. Ethylbenzene	100-41-4	7.0	100 ppm-A,O 125 ppm-A 15 min(STEL)
15. Ethylene glycol monobutyl ether acetate	112-07-2	0.3	20 ppm-D Skin None-A,O
16. Hexyl acetate isomers	88230-35-7	0.7	50 ppm-A None-O
17. Hydrous magnesium silicate	14807-96-6	None	2 mg/m³-A,O Resp
18. Iron oxide	1309-37-1	None	10 mg/m³-A None-O
19. Kaolin	58425-86-8	None	10 mg/m³-A None-O
20. Methyl amyl ketone	110-43-0	2.2	50 ppm-A 100 ppm-O
21. Methyl ethyl ketone	78-93-3	71.0	200 ppm-A,O 300 ppm-A 15 min(STEL) 200 ppm-D 8&12 hr TWA
22. Methyl isobutyl ketone	108-10-1	15.0	50 ppm-A 100 ppm-O 75 ppm-A 15 min(STEL)
23 Mixed dibasic esters	Not Available	0.2	10 mg/m³-D None-A,O
24. Polyester Resin	71010-58-7	None	None A,O
25. Propylene glycol monomethyl ether acetate	108-65-6	3.7	None-A,O 10 ppm-D
26. Quartz- crystalline silica	14808-60-7	None	0.1 mg/m³-A,O Resp
27. Low oil absorption Talc	14807-96-6	None	2 mg/m³-A,O Resp
28. Micronized titanium dioxide	13463-67-7	None	10 mg/m³-A 15 mg/m³-O 10 mg/m³-D
29. Titanium dioxide	13463-67-7	None	10 mg/m³-A 15 mg/m³-O 10 mg/m³-D
30. Toluene	108-88-3	36.7	50 ppm-A Skin 100 ppm-O 300 ppm-O Ceiling 500 ppm-O 10 min MAX
31. Xylene	1330-20-7	25.0	100 ppm-A,O 150 ppm-A,O 15 min(STEL)
32. Zinc and calcium molybdate	Not Available	None	10 mg/m³-A 15 mg/m³-O 5 mg/m³-O Resp
33. Zinc phosphate	7779-90-0	None	10 mg/m³-A 15 mg/m³-O 5 mg/m³-O Resp
34. 1,6 Hexamethylene diisocyanate	822-06-0	Unkwn	5 ppb-A None-O

A = ACGIH TLV; O= OSHA; D = DuPont internal limit; S=Supplier Furnished limit; STEL = Short Term Exposure Limit; C= Ceiling.

Section III - Physical Data

Evaporation rate: Less than ether
Vapor Density: Heavier than air
Solubility in water: Miscible
Percent volatile by volume: 29.9%- 100%
Percent volatile by weight: 24.9%- 70%
Boiling range: 0°C- 225°C /32°F- 437°F
Gallon weight: 7.30- 12.39 lbs./gallon

Section IV - Fire and Explosion Data

Flash point (closed cup): See Section X for exact values.
   Flammable limits: 0.1%- 15.3%
   Extinguishing media: Water spray, foam, carbon dioxide, dry chemical.
   Special fire fighting procedures: Full protective equipment, including self-contained breathing apparatus, is recommended. Water from fog nozzles may be used to cool closed containers to prevent pressure build up.
   Unusual fire & explosion hazards: When heated above the flash point, emits flammable vapors which, when mixed with air, can burn or be explosive. Fine mists or sprays may be flammable at temperatures below the flash point.

Section V - Health Hazard Data

General effects

Ingestion: Gastrointestinal distress. In the unlikely event of ingestion, call a physician immediately and have the names of ingredients available.

Inhalation: May cause nose and throat irritation. Repeated and prolonged overexposure to solvents may lead to permanent brain and nervous system damage. Eye watering, headaches, nausea, dizziness and loss of coordination are signs that solvent levels are too high. Exposure to isocyanates may cause respiratory sensitization. This effect may be permanent. This effect may be delayed for several hours after exposure. Repeated overexposure to isocyanates may cause a decrease in lung function which may be permanent. Individuals with or breathing problems or prior reaction to isocyanates must not be exposed to vapors or spray mist of this product. If affected by inhalation of vapor or spray mist, remove to fresh air. If breathing difficulty persists, or occurs later, consult a physician.

Skin or eye contact: May cause irritation or burning of the eyes. Repeated or prolonged liquid contact may cause skin irritation with discomfort and dermatitis. In case of eye contact, immediately flush with plenty of water for at least 15 minutes; call a physician. In case of skin contact, wash with soap and water. If irritation occurs, contact a physician.

Specific Effects:

Aliphatic polyisocyanate resin/aliphatic polymeric isocyanate/1,6-hexamethylene diisocyanate - Repeated exposure may cause allergic skin rash, itching, swelling. May cause eye irritation with discomfort, tearing, or blurred vision. Repeated overexposure to isocyanates may cause lung injury, including a decrease in lung function, which may be permanent. Overexposure may cause asthma-like reactions with shortness of breath, wheezing, cough, which may be permanent; or permanent lung sensitization. This effect may be delayed for several hours after exposure. Individuals with preexisting lung disease, asthma or breathing difficulties may have increased susceptibility to the toxicity of excessive exposures.

Aromatic Hydrocarbon A,B - Laboratory studies with rats have shown that petroleum distillates cause kidney damage and kidney or liver tumors. These effects were not seen in similar studies with guinea pigs, dogs, or monkeys. Several studies evaluating petroleum workers have not shown a significant increase of kidney damage or an increase in kidney or liver tumors. **Butyl acetate** - May cause abnormal liver function. Tests for embryotoxic activity in animals has been inconclusive. Has been toxic to the fetus in laboratory animals at doses that are toxic to the mother. **Diatomaceous Earth** - Repeated and prolonged overexposure may lead to chronic lung disease. **Ethyl acetate:** Prolonged and repeated high exposures of laboratory animals resulted in secondary anemia with and increase in white blood cells; fatty degeneration, cloudy swelling and excess of blood in various organs. **Ethylbenzene** - Recurrent overexposure may result in liver and kidney injury. Studies in laboratory animals have shown reproductive, embryotoxic and developmental effects. Has shown mu-

tagenic activity in laboratory cell culture tests. Tests in some laboratory animals demonstrate carcinogenic activity. **Ethylene glycol monobutyl ether acetate** - Can be absorbed through the skin in harmful amounts. May destroy red blood cells. May cause abnormal kidney function. **Hydrous magnesium silicate (Talc)** - Repeated and prolonged overexposure to talc may lead to typical X-ray changes and chronic lung disease. **Methyl ethyl ketone** - High concentration have caused embryotoxic effects in laboratory animals. Methyl ethyl ketone has been demonstrated to potentiate (i.e., shorten the time of onset) the peripheral neuropathy caused by either n-hexane or methyl n-butyl ketone. MEK by itself has not been demonstrated to cause peripheral neuropathy. Liquid splashes in the eye may result in chemical burns. **Methyl isobutyl ketone** - Recurrent overexposure may result in liver and kidney injury. **Mixed dibasic esters:** High airborne levels in rats have shown mild injury to the olfactory region of the nose. **Propylene glycol monomethyl ether acetate** - May cause moderate eye burning. Recurrent overexposure may result in liver and kidney injury. **Quartz-crystalline silica** - Repeated overexposure to crystalline silica may lead to typical x-ray changes and chronic lung disease. Is an IARC, NTP, or OSHA carcinogen. WARNING: This chemical is known to the State of California to cause cancer. **Titanium dioxide** - In a lifetime inhalation test, lung cancers were found in some rats exposed to 250 mg/m^3 respirable titanium dust. Analysis of the titanium dioxide concentrations in the rat's lungs showed that the lung clearance mechanism was overwhelmed and that the results at the massive 250 mg/m^3 level are not relevant to the workplace. **Toluene** - Recurrent overexposure may result in liver and kidney injury. High airborne levels have produced irregular heart beats in animals and occasional palpitations in humans. Rats exposed to very high airborne levels have exhibited high frequency hearing deficits. The significance of this to man is unknown. WARNING: This chemical is known to the State of California to cause birth defects or other reproductive harm . **Xylene** - High concentration have caused embryotoxic effects in laboratory animals. Recurrent overexposure may result in liver and kidney injury. Can be absorbed through the skin in harmful amounts. **Zinc oxide/molybdate and Zinc phosphate pigment** - Overexposure may cause eye, nose and throat irritation. Repeated or prolonged contact may cause skin irritation with discomfort and dermatitis.

Section VI - Reactivity Data

Stability: Stable
   Incompatibility (materials to avoid): None reasonably foreseeable
   Hazardous decomposition products: CO, CO_2, smoke.
   Hazardous polymerization: Will not occur.

Section VII - Spill or Leak Procedures

Steps to be taken in case material is released or spilled: Do not breathe vapors. Do not get in eyes or on skin. Wear a positive pressure supplied air vapor/particulate respirator (NIOSH/MSHA TC-19C), eye protection, gloves and protective material. Remove sources of ignition. Absorb with inert material. Ventilate area. Pour liquid decontaminate solution over the spill and allow to sit 10 minutes, minimum. Typical decontamination solutions are:

	20% Surfactant (Tergitol TMN 10)
	80% Water
or	0-10% Ammonia
	2-5% Detergent
	Balance water

This procedure can generate pressure. Do not seal containers. After 48 hours, seal container and dispose of.

Waste disposal method: Do not allow material to contaminate ground water systems. Incinerate absorbed material in accordance with federal, state, and local requirements. Do not incinerate in closed containers.

2

Section VIII - Special Protection Information

Respiratory: Do not breathe vapors or mists. Wear a positive pressure supplied air respirator (NIOSH/MSHA (TC-19C) while mixing activator with any paint or clear enamel, during application and until all vapors and spray mists are exhausted. Individuals with a history of lung or breathing problems or prior reaction to isocyanate should not use or be exposed to this product. Do not permit anyone without protection in the painting area. Follow the respirator manufacturer's directions for respirator use.

Ventilation: Provide sufficient ventilation in volume and pattern to keep contaminants below applicable OSHA requirements.

Protective clothing: Neoprene gloves and coveralls are recommended.

Eye protection: Desirable in all industrial situations. Include splash guards or side shields.

Special Precautions

Precautions to be taken in handling and storing: Observe label precautions. Keep away from heat, sparks and flame. Close container after each use. Ground containers when pouring. Wash thoroughly after handling and before eating or smoking. Do not store above 120°F.

Other precautions: Do not sand, flame cut, braze or weld dry coating without a NIOSH/MSHA approved respirator or appropriate ventilation.

Section X - Other Information

Section 313 Supplier Notification: The chemicals listed below with percentages are subject to the reporting requirements of Section 313 of the Emergency Planning and Right-To-Know Act of 1986 and of 40 CFR 372.

PRODUCT CODE   **INGREDIENTS (See Section II)**

1075S   6, 9, 19, 21, 24(6%), 25(8%), **GAL WT: 7.59 WT PCT SOLIDS: 0.00 VOL PCT SOLIDS: 0.00 SOLVENT DENSITY: 7.59 VOC: 7.5 H: 2 F: 3 R: 0 FLASH PT: -73L OSHA STORAGE: IB**

1080S   1, 6, 9, 10(8%), 18(3%), 21, 24(1%), 25(25%), **GAL WT: 7.96 WT PCT SOLIDS: 35.99 VOL PCT SOLIDS: 30.67 SOLVENT DENSITY: 7.35 VOC: 5.0 H: 2 F: 3 R: 0 FLASH PT: -100L OSHA STORAGE: IC**

1082S   2, 4, 6, 25(30%), 28, **GAL WT: 8.61 WT PCT SOLIDS: 63.00 VOL PCT SOLIDS: 55.75 SOLVENT DENSITY: 7.20 VOC: 3.1 H: 3 F: 3 R: 1 FLASH PT: -73L OSHA STORAGE: IB**

1085S   12, 21, **GAL WT: 7.78 WT PCT SOLIDS: 0.00 VOL PCT SOLIDS: 0.00 SOLVENT DENSITY: 7.78 VOC: 7.7 H: 1 F: 3 R: 0 FLASH PT: -73L OSHA STORAGE: IB**

1095S   11(20%), 12, **GAL WT: 7.37 WT PCT SOLIDS: 0.00 VOL PCT SOLIDS: 0.00 SOLVENT DENSITY: 7.37 VOC: 7.3 H: 2 F: 3 R: 0 FLASH PT: -100L OSHA STORAGE: IC**

1120S   1, 5(13%), 11(1%), 13, 14, 21, 23, 25(21%), 27(3%), **GAL WT:12.85 WT PCT SOLIDS: 69.29 VOL PCT SOLIDS: 46.50 SOLVENT DENSITY: 7.38 VOC: 3.9 H: 1 F: 3 R: 0 FLASH PT: -100L OSHA STORAGE: IC**

1125S   2, 4, 6, 9, 25(27%), **GAL WT: 8.12 WT PCT SOLIDS: 39.85 VOL PCT SOLIDS: 33.29 SOLVENT DENSITY: 7.32 VOC: 4.8 H: 3 F: 3 R: 1 FLASH PT: -73L/ OSHA STORAGE: IB**

1130S   4, 6, 9, 24(20%), 25(24%), **GAL WT: 7.26 WT PCT SOLIDS: 0.06 VOL PCT SOLIDS: 0.05 SOLVENT DENSITY: 7.26 VOC: 7.2 H: 2 F: 3 R: 0 FLASH PT: -73L OSHA STORAGE: IB**

1135S   4, 6, 9, 24(18%), 25(21%), **GAL WT: 7.28 WT PCT SOLIDS: 0.16 VOL PCT SOLIDS: 0.13 SOLVENT DENSITY: 7.28 VOC: 7.2 H: 2 F: 3 R: 0 FLASH PT: -73L OSHA STORAGE: IB**

1140S   1, 5(13%), 11(1%), 13, 21, 23, 25(21%), 27, **GAL WT: 12.87 WT PCT SOLIDS: 69.29 VOL PCT SOLIDS: 46.40 SOLVENT DENSITY: 7.37 VOC: 3.9 H: 1 F: 3 R: 0 FLASH PT: -100L OSHA STORAGE: IC**

1220S   1, 7, 8, 9, 11(6%), 13, 15, 16, 17(16%), 22(3%), 23, 25(2%), 26(3%), **GAL WT: 10.82 WT PCT SOLIDS: 63.79 VOL PCT SOLIDS: 44.03 SOLVENT DENSITY: 7.00 VOC: 3.9 H: 2 F: 3 R: 0 FLASH PT: -73L OSHA STORAGE: IB**

2080S   1, 9, 17(11%), 21, 24(6%) **GAL WT: 8.06 WT PCT SOLIDS: 29.93 VOL PCT SOLIDS: 25.19 SOLVENT DENSITY: 7.40 VOC: 5.6 H:2 F:3 R:0 FLASH PT: -73L OSHA STORAGE: IB**

2082S   3, 6, 9, 11(4%), 17(1%), 28, **GAL WT: 8.99 WT PCT SOLIDS: 75.14 VOL PCT SOLIDS: 70.01 SOLVENT DENSITY: 7.45 VOC: 2.2 H: 3 F: 3 R: 1 FLASH PT: -73L OSHA STORAGE: IB**

2085S   1, 9, 17(11%), 20, 21, 24(68%), **GAL WT: 8.06 WT PCT SOLIDS: 29.96 VOL PCT SOLIDS: 25.21 SOLVENT DENSITY: 7.55 VOC: 5.6 H: 2 F: 3 R: 0 FLASH PT: -73L OSHA STORAGE: IB**

Notice: The data in this material safety data sheet relate only to the specific material designated herein and do not relate to use in combination with any other material or in any process.

Product Manager - Refinish Sales

Rev. 1/95
Prepared by T.R. Louer, CIH
(302) 774-8303

Job Sheet 1-1

Name_____ Date _____ Instructor Review _____

Equipment Operation

Objective

After completing this lab, the student should be able to operate overhead doors, lifts, floor jacks, and spray booths.

Equipment

Your instructor will demonstrate how to operate the following equipment:

1. Overhead doors
2. Lift
3. Floor jack and jack stands
4. Spray booth

Safety Equipment

Safety glasses

Procedure

Answer the following questions with a paragraph explanation.

1. How do you operate the overhead doors? _____

   _____

   _____

2. You need to raise a unibody car on the lift. How do you do it? _____

   _____

   _____

3. What is the procedure to safely raise the rear end of a pick-up truck with a floor jack and jack stands? _____

   _____

   _____

4. Diagram the air flow in your school's spray booth. List the procedural steps in use.

   _____

   _____

   _____

   _____

Review Questions

Name_____ Date _____ Instructor Review _____

1. A damaged vehicle is _____ when repair costs are greater than the vehicle value.

2. The two major work areas in any body shop are _____ and

   _____.

3. Technician A says that frame work requires careful measuring. Technician B believes that frame work requires clamping the vehicle in place. Who is correct?

   A. Technician A
   B. Techician B
   C. Both A and B
   D. Neither A nor B

4. When painting a vehicle, Technician A masks off emblems. Technician B removes the emblems. Who is correct?

   A. Technician A
   B. Techician B
   C. Both A and B
   D. Neither A nor B

5. Technician A checks the VIN to determine the model year. Technician B checks the VIN to determine the engine type. Who is correct?

   A. Technician A
   B. Techician B
   C. Both A and B
   D. Neither A nor B

6. _____ refers to anything that prevents normal breathing.

7. Technician A wears a respirator when spraying paint. Technician B wears a dust mask when spraying paint. Who is correct?

   A. Technician A
   B. Techician B
   C. Both A and B
   D. Neither A nor B

8. Technician A states that testing a respirator for fit requires negative and positive tests. Technician B believes that a beard prevents proper respirator fit. Who is correct?

   A. Technician A
   B. Techician B
   C. Both A and B
   D. Neither A nor B

9. Flammable liquids cause a Type _____ fire.

10. Lead, cadmium and arsenic are considered hazardous because of their _____

    _____.

Chapter 2
Understanding Automobile Construction

Shop Assignment 2-1

Name_____ Date _____ Instructor Review _____

Information Labels

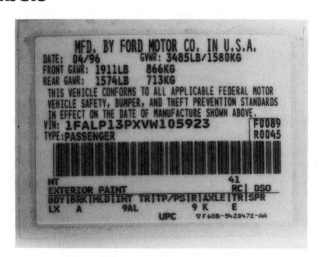

1. What is the VIN? _____
2. Using a crash estimating guide, answer the following questions:
   A. What is the vehicle model year? _____
   B. What is the engine size? _____
   C. Where was the car assembled? _____
   D. What is the body type? _____
   E. What is the type of restraint system? _____
3. What is the body code?_____
4. What is the paint code?_____
5. Where is this label found on the car? _____

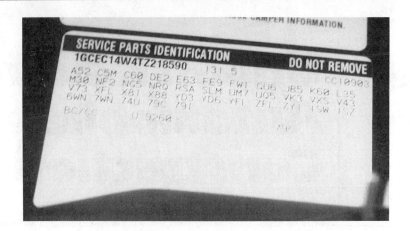

1. What is the VIN? _____

2. Using a crash estimating guide, answer the following questions:

   A. What is the GVWR? _____

   B. What is the engine size? _____

   C. What is the vehicle model year? _____

   D. What is the chassis type? _____

   E. What is the nation of origin? _____

3. What is the paint code? _____

4. Where is this label found on the truck? _____

1. What is the VIN? _____

2. Using a crash estimating guide, answer the following questions:

   A. What is the vehicle type? _____

   B. What is the engine size? _____

   C. What is the model year? _____

   D. What is the body type? _____

   E. What is the sequential production number? _____

3. What is the paint code? _____

4. Where is this label found on the vehicle? _____

Shop Assignment 2-2

Name_____ Date _____ Instructor Review _____

Vehicle Parts

1. What type of frame does the car have?_____

2. Write the number for each part beside the name.

_____	A pillar		_____	rear bumper
_____	fender		_____	right rear door
_____	front bumper		_____	sail panel
_____	quarter panel		_____	right front door
_____	B pillar		_____	C Pillar
_____	right front wheel		_____	right rear wheel

_____	front bumper		_____	header panel
_____	grille		_____	windshield
_____	head light		_____	hood

_____ back glass

_____ tail light

_____ rear body panel

_____ rear bumper

_____ high stop lamp

_____ license plate light

3. What type of frame does this vehicle have? _____

4. Write the number for each part beside the name.

_____ cab   _____ right front wheel

_____ cab corner   _____ right door

_____ right fender   _____ rocker panel

_____ right bedside   _____ windshield pillar

_____ right rear wheel

Shop Assignment 2-3

Name_____ Date _____ Instructor Review _____

Mechanical Components

Label the diagrams and answer the questions.

1. Steering systems

    A.

    _____ steering gear box   _____ tie rod end

    _____ pitman arm   _____ idler arm

    _____ center link   _____ steering arm

    Is this a power steering system? _____

    What type of steering system is this?_____

    B.

    _____ gear assembly   _____ steering arm

    _____ boot   _____ outer tie rod

    What type of steering system is this?_____

2. Suspension systems

A.

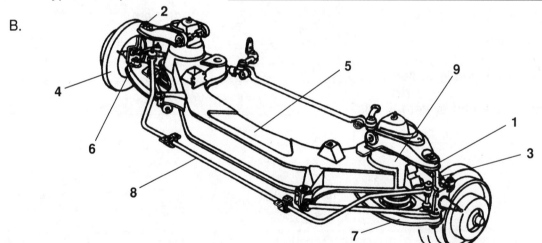

_____	strut	_____	spring
_____	ball joint	_____	hub
_____	stabilizer bar	_____	strut rod
_____	control arm		

What type of suspension is this? _____

B.

_____	brake rotor	_____	lower control arm
_____	frame	_____	stabilizer
_____	steering knuckle	_____	upper ball joint
_____	shock absorber	_____	lower ball joint
_____	upper control arm		

What type of suspension is this? _____

3. Drive train components

A.

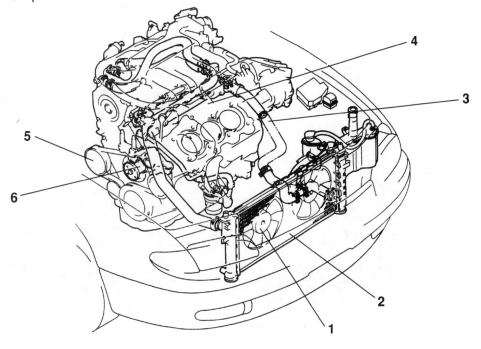

What type of drive train is this? _____

_____ radiator	_____ water pump
_____ radiator fan	_____ pulley
_____ radiator hose	_____ engine

B.

What type of drive train is this? _____

_____ inner CV joint	_____ transmission
_____ outer CV joint	_____ steering knuckle
_____ drive axle	

C.

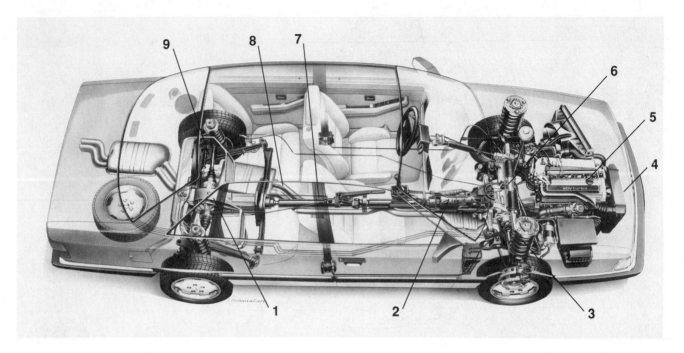

What type of drive train is this? _____

_____ radiator

_____ engine

_____ transmission

_____ strut

_____ rack and pinion

_____ drive shaft

_____ rear axle housing

_____ drive axle

_____ exhaust pipe

Review Questions

Name_____ Date _____ Instructor Review _____

1. Technician A says that most trucks have a body over frame. Technician B states that most front wheel drive cars are unibody. Who is correct?

   A. Technician A
   B. Techician B
   C. Both A and B
   D. Neither A nor B

2. Technician A states that a sedan has a center pillar and a hardtop does not have any center pillar. Technician B states that sport utility vehicles can be two wheel or four wheel drive. Who is correct?

   A. Technician A
   B. Techician B
   C. Both A and B
   D. Neither A nor B

3. The front clip is also called a _____

   _____ .

4. The quarter panels, rear floor pan, rear frame rails, deck lid, and rear bumper are also called the _____

   _____ .

5. The front doors are welded to or bolted to the _____ .

6. Ultra high strength steel is used to make

   _____ .

7. A damaged unibody vehicle requires a more thorough damage analysis than a conventional frame/body car.

   A. True
   B. False

8. Technician A states that "FR" means front engine, rear wheel drive. Technician B believes that "FR" means front engine, front wheel drive. Who is correct?

   A. Technician A
   B. Techician B
   C. Both A and B
   D. Neither A nor B

9. The post mounted on the body that engages the door latch is called the

   _____ .

10. Both metal and plastic parts can be adhesive bonded.

    A. True
    B. False

Shop Assignment 3-1

Name_____ Date _____ Instructor Review _____

Hand Tool Identification

1. Hammers—For each type of hammer, give the name and explain the situation in which it is used.

a) Name _____
   Use _____

b) Name _____
   Use _____

c) Name _____
   Use _____

d) Name _____
   Use _____

e) Name _____
   Use _____

f) Name _____
   Use _____

2. Dollies—For each type of dolly, give the name and explain what type of panel it can be used to repair.

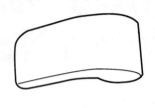

a) Name _____   b) Name _____   c) Name _____

   Panel _____   Panel _____   Panel_____

3. Spoons—For each spoon, give the name and the use.

a) Name _____   b) Name _____   c) Name _____

   Use _____   Use_____   Use _____

4. Pullers—For each type of puller, give the name and the use.

a) Name _____   b) Name _____   c) Name _____

   Use _____   Use_____   Use _____

5. Sanders—For each type of sander, give the name and the use.

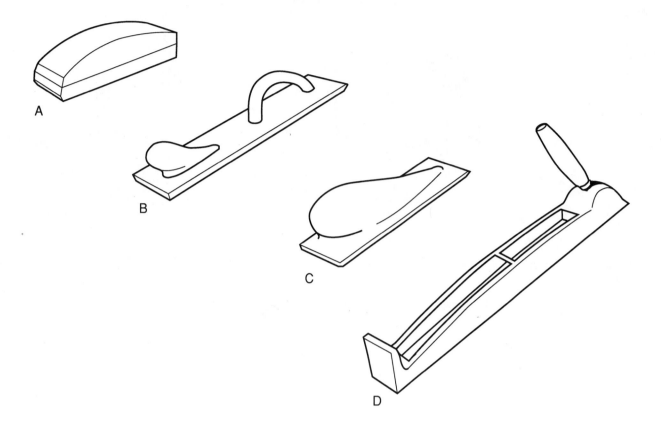

A

B

C

D

a) Name _____   b) Name _____

   Use _____   Use _____

c) Name _____   d) Name _____

   Use _____   Use _____

Job Sheet 3-1

Name_____ Date _____ Instructor Review _____

Hammer and Dolly Use

Objective

After completing this lab, the student should be able to use a hammer and dolly.

Equipment

Pick hammer
Fender
Dollies
Ruler

Safety Equipment

Safety glasses

Procedure

Hammer

See page 250 in your textbook for an explanation of how to use the hammer.

Task Completed

1. Make a series of 1/2" diameter circles in a painted panel. ❏

2. Use a sharp pick hammer to hit inside the circle. ❏

3. Practice until you can consistently hit 9 out of 10 tries inside the circle. ❏

4. Make a series of 1/4" diameter circles in a painted panel. ❏

5. Use the pick hammer to hit inside the circle as before. Practice until you can consistently hit 9 out of 10 tries inside the circle. ❏

6. Make a series of X's in a painted panel. ❏

7. Practice hitting the intersection of the "X". ❏

8. Draw a 2" x 2" sqaure on a painted panel. ❏

9. Practice hitting all the way around the square. ❏

10. Use the pick hammer to make a 2" x 2" square in the panel. No drawing ahead of time. ❏

11. Draw a 1/2" diameter circle in a painted panel. ❏

12. Using the hammer from the inside is known as *blind picking.* Hit inside the circle. Practice until you can consistently hit 9 out of 10 tries inside the circle. ❏

13. Draw a 1/4" diameter circle in a painted panel. ❏

14. Practice blind picking until you can consistently hit 9 out of 10 tries inside the circle. ❏

Dolly

1. Match all surfaces on a universal dolly to the contour of several panels. ❏

2. Place a dolly on the inside of a panel. Practice locating the dolly with a hammer. ❏

Job Sheet 3-2

Name_____ Date _____ Instructor Review _____

Files and Sanders

Objective

After completing this lab, the student should be able to use files and sanders.

Equipment

File
Pick hammer
#80, #220 grit paper
Long board sander
Sanding block
Scrap fender

Safety Equipment

Safety glasses
Dust respirator
Leather gloves

Procedure

**Task
Completed**

1. On a painted medium crown panel, use a pick hammer to make a series of taps on the inside and outside of the panel.   ❑

2. Adjust the body file to match the panel contour, using the turn buckle.   ❑

3. See page 240 in your textbook. Stroke the file at a 30- to 45-degree angle five times in one direction and five times in the opposite direction.   ❑

4. Identify these areas:
   Bare metal—high spots   ❑
   Painted—low spots   ❑

5. Prepare another panel in the same manner.   ❑

6. Sand at a 30- to 45-degree angle using a long board with #80 grit paper. Stroke 10 times in one direction and 10 times in the opposite direction. Note highs and lows.   ❑

7. Prepare another panel in the same manner.   ❑

8. Sand at a 30- to 45-degree angle using a sanding block with 220 grit paper. Stroke 20 times in one direction and 20 times in the opposite direction. Note the highs and lows.   ❑

Job Sheet 3-3

Name_____ Date _____ Instructor Review _____

Make a Body Filler Board

Objective

After completing this lab, the student should have a useable body filler board.

Equipment

20 gauge sheet metal
Scribe
Hole saw
Tin snips
Ruler
Sheet metal brake
Rat tail file

Safety Equipment

Safety glasses

Procedure

	Task Completed
1. Cut out a 12" x 12" sheet of 20 gauge sheet metal.	❑
2. Measure and scribe a line 1" from the edges.	❑
3. Cut out the corners with tin snips.	❑
4. Use a sheet metal brake to bend on the lines.	❑
5. Cut out a 2" diameter hole in one corner.	❑
6. Use the rat tail file to remove the sharp edges from the hole.	❑

Review Questions

Name_____ Date _____ Instructor Review _____

1. Technician A buys tools with a lifetime warranty. Technician B buys the cheapest tools he can find. Who is correct?

   A. Technician A
   B. Techician B
   C. Both A and B
   D. Neither A nor B

2. Technician A uses an adjustable wrench on all nuts. Technician B uses a combination wrench when possible. Who is correct?

   A. Technician A
   B. Techician B
   C. Both A and B
   D. Neither A nor B

3. A _____ inch long pipe wrench is adequate for most body shop applications.

4. A torx fastener is also called a _____

   _____ .

5. Technician A states that a socket and rachet is faster than a wrench. Technican B believes a wrench is faster than a socket and rachet. Who is correct?

   A. Technician A
   B. Techician B
   C. Both A and B
   D. Neither A nor B

6. Technician A states that a slotted head screw slips less during removal than a Phillips screw. Technician B believes that a Phillips slips less. Who is correct?

   A. Technician A
   B. Techician B
   C. Both A and B
   D. Neither A nor B

7. Technician A uses a small slotted screw driver to turn a Phillips head screw. Technician B uses a Phillips screw driver only to turn a Phillips head screw. Who is correct?

   A. Technician A
   B. Techician B
   C. Both A and B
   D. Neither A nor B

8. Adjustable pliers are also called _____

   _____ .

9. Vise grips can be used for clamping metal together and for turning rounded off fasteners.

   A. True
   B. False

10. Technician A uses a cheater pipe to help turn off a rusted nut. Technician B heats the nut and then turns it off with a rachet. Who is correct?

    A. Technician A
    B. Techician B
    C. Both A and B
    D. Neither A nor B

Chapter 4

Body Shop Power Tools

Shop Assignment 4-1

Name_____ Date _____ Instructor Review _____

Power Tool Identification Lab

1. Power Tools—For each type of power tool, give the name and explain the situation in which it is used.

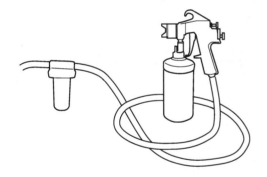

a) Name _____   b) Name _____   c) Name_____

   Uos_____   Uses _____   Uses _____

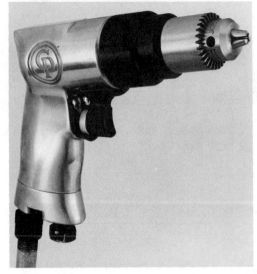  

d) Name _____

Uses _____

e) Name _____

Uses _____

f) Name _____

Uses _____

g) Name _____

Uses _____

h) Name _____

Uses _____

i) Name _____

Uses _____

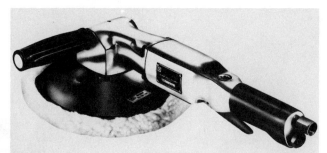

j) Name_____

   Uses_____

k) Name _____

   Uses _____

l) Name _____

   Uses_____

m) Name_____

   Uses _____

n) Name _____

   Uses_____

o) Name _____

   Uses _____

p) Name _____   q) Name _____   r) Name _____

Uses _____   Uses _____   Uses _____

s) Name _____   t) Name _____

Uses _____   Uses _____

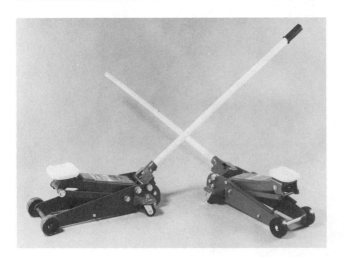

u) Name _____

   Uses _____

v) Name _____

   Uses _____

w) Name _____

   Uses _____

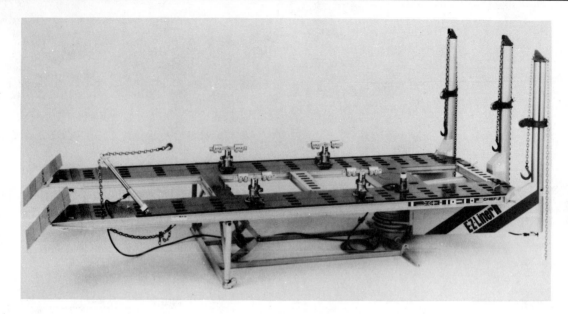

x) Name _____

   Uses _____

Job Sheet 4-1

Name_____ Date _____ Instructor Review _____

Power Tool Operation

Objective

After completing this lab, the student should be able to safely use a grinder, an air file, a jitterbug, and a dual-action sander.

Equipment

Grinder
Jitterbug
Painted fender
Air file
Dual-action sander

Safety Equipment

Safety glasses
Dust respirator
Leather gloves

Procedure

For safe operation of these tools, always:

1. Check the condition of the pad, disk, or paper before operation. If any paint buildup, nicks, tears, or holes are found, make the necessary repairs.

2. Stop the tool on the panel. Do not hold a running grinder in the air.

Obtain a Painted Fender.

1. Grinder

   A. Buff to remove the paint (see page 249). With both hands, hold the grinder at a slight angle and grind three inches in one direction. Move down and grind below the first pass. This removes the paint. Do not grind any longer than necessary. If the panel turns blue, you've ground too long. ❑

   B. Cross cut to remove the metal. Tap a few high spots in the fender. Remove them by grinding in one direction. Then go back over the same area. Do not overheat the panel. ❑

   C. For a concave surface, grind off the paint using the buffing technique. Note the deep gouges. Cut out a disk as shown on page 249 in your textbook. Grind paint off of another concave area. Compare the areas. Which method is preferred and why? ❑

   D. If you have not yet made metal turn blue by the heat of the grinder, do it now. In the same cases, this can be used in dent repair. ❑

Task Completed

2. Air file
    Use #24 or #36 grit paper on an air file to remove the paint from an area at
    least 12" x 3". Hold the file flat against the panel. Do not turn it up on edge.   ❏

3. Jitterbug
    Use #80 grit paper on a jitterbug to smooth down the deep scratches in the
    bare metal, as well as to featheredge the paint. Hold the jitterbug flat against   ❏
    the panel.

4. Dual-action sander
    Use #180 grit paper on a finish dual-action sander to continue featheredging
    on the panel. Hold the dual-action sander flat to the panel. Move it slowly.   ❏
    Stop when you have one inch of each paint layer showing.

Review Questions

Name_____ Date _____ Instructor Review _____

1. The advantage of air tools over electric tools are flexibility, lighter weight, _____ and

_____.

2. Technician A uses only impact sockets on his impact wrench. Technician B believes that for small bolts, a chrome socket is an acceptable choice to use on an impact wrench. Who is correct?

   A. Technician A
   B. Techician B
   C. Both A and B
   D. Neither A nor B

3. Technician A uses an impact wrench to final torque a fastener. Technician B uses a torque wrench. Who is correct?

   A. Technician A
   B. Techician B
   C. Both A and B
   D. Neither A nor B

4. The "walking" of a spinning drill can be prevented by first using a _____

_____.

5. Which type of spot weld cutter bit does not leave a nib in the bottom panel.

   A. Drill type
   B. Hole saw type

6. The two basic types of air sanders are _____ and

_____.

7. Technician A uses an inline oiler on all air lines. Technician B uses the oiler on all lines except those used for painting. Who is correct?

   A. Technician A
   B. Techician B
   C. Both A and B
   D. Neither A nor B

8. Technician A uses a heat gun to repair plastic. Technician B uses a heat gun to dry paint. Who is correct?

   A. Technician A
   B. Techician B
   C. Both A and B
   D. Neither A nor B

9. The three parts of a hydraulic jack are

_____,

_____

and _____.

10. Which lift is best for estimating body damage?

   A. Four post and two post
   B. Side post
   C. Center post

Compressed Air Supply Equipment

Job Sheet 5-1

Name_____ Date _____ Instructor Review _____

Air Compressor System

Objective

After completing this lab, the student should have an understanding of the air compressor system in his school's shop.

Equipment	**Safety Equipment**
Air compressor system	Safety glasses
Air pressure gauge	

Procedure

1. Make an outline drawing of a shop air system. In the diagram, include the following:

Air compressor	Driers
Air lines—Indicate diameter	Water traps
Air transformers	Air hoses
Filters	

2. What is the line pressure at each air transformer?

    Transformer   Line Pressure

    _____   _____

    _____   _____

    _____   _____

3. Attach a 25-foot air hose to an air transformer. Measure the air pressure at the end of the
    hose. _____

    _____

    Read the air pressure at the transformer. _____

    Why is there a difference? _____

    _____

4. Make a drawing of your school's air compressor. In your diagram, indicate the following:
    Air intake
    Cylinders
    Electric motor
    Tank (indicate size)
    Pressure cut-off switch
    Pressure gauge
    Tank drain
    Drive belt

5. Your instructor will explain how to do the following:

Change the compressor oil

Adjust the drive belt

Set the cut-off pressure

Summarize each of these tasks in separate paragraphs. _____

_____

_____

_____

_____

_____

_____

_____

_____

_____

_____

_____

_____

6. Your instructor will explain how to replace a damaged hose end.

Summarize the procedure in a paragraph. _____

_____

_____

_____

_____

_____

_____

_____

_____

_____

_____

_____

_____

Review Questions

Name_____ Date _____ Instructor Review _____

1. The three types of air compressors are

   _____,

   _____ and

   _____.

2. Which compressor is most efficient?

   A. Single stage
   B. Two stage

3. Which is the best rating to use when selecting an air compressor?

   A. Displacement CFM
   B. Free air CFM

4. Air compressor tanks can be mounted vertically or _____.

5. Technician A drains the air compressor tank each day. Technician B drains the air compressor tank each month. Who is correct?

   A. Technician A
   B. Technician B
   C. Both A and B
   D. Neither A nor B

6. The _____ starts and stops the compressor motor based on the system pressure.

7. An air transformer is also called a _____

   _____.

8. Elimination of oil, dirt, and moisture in air lines is provided by a_____.

9. Technician A uses an after cooler to remove moisture. Technician B believes that the after cooler removes oil. Who is correct?

   A. Technician A
   B. Technician B
   C. Both A and B
   D. Neither A nor B

10. A ¼" hose is acceptable for all uses in a body shop.

   A. True
   B. False

Chapter 6

Auto Body Materials and Fasteners

Shop Assignment 6-1

Name_____ Date _____ Instructor Review _____

Paint System

Obtain the shop manual for the brand of paint you will use. Complete the following chart with the information found in the manual. List all part numbers if the material is two or three part.

Materials	Part Numbers	Use
1. Self etching primer	_____	_____
2. Epoxy primer	_____	_____
3. Filler primer	_____	_____
4. Acrylic lacquer	_____	_____
5. Acrylic enamel	_____	_____
6. Single stage urethane	_____	_____
7. BC/CC urethane base coat	_____	_____
8. BC/CC urethane clear coat	_____	_____
9. Sealer	_____	_____
10. Waterborne primer	_____	_____

Shop Assignment 6-2

Name_____ Date _____ Instructor Review _____

Sandpaper Grits

List the grit paper you would use to do the following tasks:

Task	**Sandpaper Grit**
1. Sand OEM paint	_____
2. Sand large body filler area	_____
3. Strip paint	_____
4. Sand primer	_____
5. Color sand	_____
6. Sand, body filler high spots	_____
7. Wet sand before polish	_____
8. Sand bare metal	_____
9. Final sand body filler	_____
10. Featheredge paint	_____

Review Questions

Name_____ Date _____ Instructor Review _____

1. Technician A states that primer improves the adhesion of the top coat. Technician B believes that the primer prevents bleed through. Who is correct?

   A. Technician A
   B. Technician B
   C. Both A and B
   D. Neither A nor B

2. _____ paint dries by chemical change.

3. The four components of paint are pigments, binders, _____, and _____.

4. Enamels are thinned; lacquers are reduced.

   A. True
   B. False

5. Technician A uses a retarder under cool shop conditions. Technician B uses an accelerator under these same conditions. Who is correct?

   A. Technician A
   B. Technician B
   C. Both A and B
   D. Neither A nor B

6. Wearing a NIOSH approved supplied air respirator is required when spraying a paint containing isocyanates.

   A. True
   B. False

7. Technician A uses a self-etching primer over bare metal. Technician B uses an epoxy primer over bare metal. Who is correct?

   A. Technician A
   B. Technician B
   C. Both A and B
   D. Neither A nor B

8. Technician A uses two part putty over primed filler. Technician B uses two part putty over bare metal. Who is correct?

   A. Technician A
   B. Technician B
   C. Both A and B
   D. Neither A nor B

9. _____ grit paper is used to first sand filler.

10. Technician A lubricates bolts before torqueting them. Technician B believes that pop rivets can be used from one side only. Who is correct?

    A. Technician A
    B. Technician B
    C. Both A and B
    D. Neither A nor B

Chapter 7

Welding Equipment and Its Use

Job Sheet 7-1

Name_____ Date _____ Instructor Review _____

MIG Welding

Objective

After completing this lab, the student should be able to use a MIG welder.

Equipment

MIG welder

Safety Equipment

Safety glasses
Welding helmet with #10 shade
Welding gloves
Welding sleeves
Welding respirator
High-top shoes

Procedure

1. Make an outline drawing of your school's MIG welder. Label the following parts:
   Gun, spool, cable ground clamp, power cord, heat adjustment knob, wire speed adjustment knob, gas bottle, and regulator.

2. Examine the gun. Remove the nozzle and contact tip. Make a drawing of the gun. Label the following parts:
   Nozzle, contact tip, neck, trigger, gas diffuser, and liner.

3. Your instructor will demonstrate how to change the spool and set tension on the wire feed. Summarize below on how these are done. Fill out the chart.

Drive Roller Tension	**Problem**
Too tight	_____
Too loose	_____

4. Your instructor will demonstrate the proper way to hold the gun. Consult Table 7–3 in your textbook for the proper speed to move the gun. Select a thickness and practice proper gun speed in both push and pull movements.

5. Fill out this chart on different welding problems:

Voltage	**Penetration**	**Bead**
Too high	_____	_____
Too low	_____	_____
Right setting	_____	_____

Wire Speed	**Sound**	**Light**
Too fast	_____	_____
Too slow	_____	_____
Right setting	_____	_____

6. List, in proper order, the steps in setting up the MIG welder for use. _____

_____

_____

_____

_____

7. Fill out this chart on weld problems:

Problem	**How to Correct**
Burn through	_____
Lack of penetration	_____
Warpage	_____

Explain how to test a weld. _____

_____

_____

_____

Weld a Bead

**Task
Completed**

8. Obtain a 12" x 12" piece of 18 gauge sheet metal. Lay it flat on a weld table. Attach a ground clamp to the piece. Set the gas flow and voltage. Put on your helmet and gloves. Trigger the gun. With proper stickout, move the gun at the correct speed. Adjust the wire speed until a steady hiss is heard. The welder is now tuned.   ❑

9. Tightly clamp a piece of 12" x 6" sheet metal to the original piece. Hold the gun at a 70 degree angle. Run a bead along the edge to form a lap joint.   ❑

10. Examine the weld. Summarize how to test welds in the space below. Perform a test on this weld. If it does not pass, continue making this weld until it is correct. _____   ❑

_____

_____

Job Sheet 7-2

Name_____ Date _____ Instructor Review _____

Flat Welds

Objective

After completing this lab, the student should be able to make a lap, plug, and butt joints with insert on flat panels.

Equipment

Weld coupons
Weld stand
MIG welder
$1/8$" thick metal
Weld clamps

Safety Equipment

Safety glasses
Welding helmet with #10 shade
Welding gloves
Welding sleeves
Welding respirator
High-top shoes

Procedure

Task Completed

1. Lap Weld
   Overlap two weld coupons. Clamp them together tightly. Adjust and tune the welder. Follow the sequence for skip welding on page 195 in your textbook. Make a $3/4$" bead at the center of the overlap. Allow the weld to cool. Weld another $3/4$" bead in the opposite direction. Then go back and continue the first weld. Follow this sequence until the entire length is welded. Test the weld. If it is not acceptable, practice until the welds are good.   ❑

2. Plug Weld
   Punch ten $5/16$" holes in a weld coupon. Overlaps this coupon onto another coupon. Clamp the two coupons together. Adjust and tune the welder. To make this weld, hold the gun at a 90 degree angle and start at the edge of the hole. Weld the edge of the top panel to the bottom panel. Evaluate the appearance and test the weld.   ❑

3. Butt Joint with Insert
   Place a coupon on the weld table. Place two coupons edge to edge with a $1/16$" gap between them. Clamp the coupons together. Place a tack weld at the center and on each edge. Then weld using the skip technique. Examine and test the weld.   ❑

4. Weld Different Thicknesses
   To weld different thicknesses, you must heat up the thicker piece and not burn through the thinner piece. This level of skill takes considerable practice. Punch two plug holes into a coupon and clamp it on a $1/8$" thick piece of steel. Adjust and tune the welder on the thick piece. Weld the hole by heating the thick piece more than the outer piece. Next drill ten $5/16$" holes into the $1/8$" thick piece. Clamp to a coupon. Adjust and tune the welder on the thin piece. Weld the hole. Do not burn through the thin piece; direct the heat to the thick hole.   ❑

Job Sheet 7-3

Name_____ Date _____ Instructor Review _____

Vertical Welds

Objective

After completing this lab, the student should be able to make a lap, plug, and butt joints with insert on a vertical panel.

Equipment

Weld coupons
Weld stand
MIG welder
Weld clamps

Safety Equipment

Safety glasses
Welding helmet with #10 shade
Welding gloves
Welding sleeves
Welding respirator
High-top shoes

Procedure

Task Completed

1. Lap Weld
   Clamp two coupons to a welding stand so the joint is vertical. Adjust and tune the welder. Skip weld the joint, always moving the gun downward. Examine and test the weld.   ❏

2. Plug Weld
   Punch ten plug weld holes in a coupon. Overlap onto another coupon. Clamp the coupons in a welding stand. Adjust and tune the welder. Plug weld the holes. Examine and test the weld.   ❏

3. Butt Joint with Insert
   Arrange three coupons, one underneath the other two. The butt joint should have a $1/16$" gap. Clamp this into a weld stand. Adjust and tune the welder. Tack weld at the center and each end. Skip weld, working out from the center, always pulling down on the gun. Examine and test the weld.   ❏

Job Sheet 7-4

Name_____ Date _____ Instructor Review _____

Overhead Welds

Objective

After completing this lab, the student should be able to make a lap, plug, and butt joints with insert on an overhead panel.

Equipment

Weld coupons
Weld stand
MIG welder
Weld clamps

Safety Equipment

Safety glasses
Welding helmet with #10 shade
Welding gloves
Welding sleeves
Welding respirator
High-top shoes

Procedure

Task Completed

1. Lap
   Clamp two coupons in the overhead position on the welding stand. These overhead welds will require lower voltage and shorter arc length. Adjust and tune the welder. Use the skip technique and pull the gun. Examine and test the weld.   ❏

2. Plug
   Punch plug holes in one coupon and overlap it on another coupon. Clamp it into the weld stand. Adjust and tune the welder. Weld the holes. Examine and test the weld.   ❏

3. Butt Joint with Insert
   Arrange three coupons and clamp in the overhead position. Adjust and tune the welder. Tack weld at the center and on either edge. Skip weld. Examine and test the weld.   ❏

Job Sheet 7-5

Name_____ Date _____ Instructor Review _____

Weld A Truck Frame

Objective

After completing this lab, the student should be able to repair cracked frame rails.

Equipment

200 amp MIG welder
30" section of U channel frame rail
Cut off tool
035 wire
Vise
Drill
$1/4$" bit
Grinder

Safety Equipment

Safety glasses
Welding helmet with #10 shade
Welding gloves
Welding sleeves
Welding respirator
High-top shoes

Procedure

Task Completed

1. Cut off a 12" piece of the frame rail using a cut off tool. Cut down the center so you end up with two L-shaped pieces. These are the reinforcements. ❏

2. Place one of the reinforcements in a vise and round off the sharp corners with a grinder. ❏

3. On the inside of the 18" rail, mark the center of one flange. Extend the mark from one edge to the center of the flange. This simulates a crack. ❏

4. Drill a $1/4$" hole, $1/2$" beyond the end of the simulated crack. ❏

5. Use the cut off wheel to make a slot with thirty degree beveled sides on the simulated crack. The base of the slot should have a gap of at least $1/16$ of an inch. ❏

6. Fit up the reinforcement. There should be six inches of reinforcement on either side of the crack. Drill holes as needed for clearance of the bolt holes or rivets. Clean up the area around the crack, inside the reinforcement and the outside of the rail. ❏

7. Set up and tune the welder. Practice beads on the unused reinforcement. ❏

8. Clamp the reinforcement in place and weld the slot first. Weld the reinforcement to the rail. Use continuous weld. ❏

9. Weld around the reinforcement edge. Continuous weld may be used. ❏

10. Use a grinder to dress welds level with surrounding surfaces. Grind only in the weld, not the reinforcement or the rail. ❏

Job Sheet 7-6

Name_____ Date _____ Instructor Review _____

Oxyacetylene Torch

Objective

After completing this lab, the student should be able to heat and cut with an oxyacetylene torch.

Equipment

Oxyacetylene cutting torch
Busted on bumper bolts
Spark lighter
Hammer
Welding face shield
Socket and rachet
Welding gloves

Safety Equipment

Safety glasses
Welding tinted face shield
Long sleeves
High-top shoes

Procedure

Task Completed

1. Examine the area to be heated. There should not be any electrical wires, gas lines, undercoat or flammable materials in the way. There should also be room for you to be out from under the heated area. Do not heat gas or fluid-filled isolators. ❏

2. Your instructor will demonstrate how to turn on the gas valves and light the torch. Set the gauges at 8 to 25 P.S.I. for oxygen and 3 to 8 P.S.I. for acetylene. Open the acetylene valve and use a spark lighter to ignite the torch. Slowly open the oxygen valve. Adjust the flame. ❏

3. Crawl underneath the car. Keep the torch pointed away from you and everything else! ❏

4. Keep the torch about one inch from the nut. Heat the nut until it glows red. ❏

5. Turn off the torch and set it out of the way. ❏

6. Put the socket and rachet on the nut. Try to turn it. ❏

7. If the nut does not turn, then relight the torch. ❏

8. Heat the nut again. Now pull the oxygen trigger. This will throw sparks as it cuts. Be sure to be out of the way. Cut the nut off at the base. ❏

9. Turn off the torch and set it aside. Tap the bolt off with a hammer. ❏

Job Sheet 7-7

Name_____ Date _____ Instructor Review _____

Plasma Cutter

Objective

After completing this lab, the student should be able to set up and safely operate a plasma cutter.

Equipment

Plasma cutter
Bare 2' x 2' sheet metal
Face shield
Saw horses

Safety Equipment

Safety glasses
Welding tinted face shield
Long sleeves
High-top shoes

**Task
Completed**

Procedure

1. Read over the plasma cutter directions. Familiarize yourself with the controls. ❑
2. Plug in the electrical line and air line. Put on the face shield. ❑
3. Set a piece of sheet metal on saw horses. Place the work clamp on the sheet metal. ❑
4. Push the nozzle into the metal. Pull the trigger. Move fast enough to cut the metal without warping the panel. When you reach the end, release the trigger. ❑
5. Draw a 3" x 3" square on the panel. Cut out the square with the torch. ❑
6. Make a 24" long straight cut by clamping a straight edge to the sheet metal. Follow the straight edge with the nozzle. ❑
7. Make a 2" diameter circle. Cut out with a torch. ❑
8. Lay out another sheet of metal over the original piece. Cut them together. ❑

Job Sheet 7-8

Name_____ Date _____ Instructor Review _____

Welding Aluminum

Objective

After completing this lab, the student should be able to weld aluminum with a MIG welder. Aluminum and its alloys differ from mild steel in that there is no color change as the temperature from welding increases. Aluminum also develops a refractory oxide when exposed to air. Although material of 0.040 inch can be MIG welded, $3/16$ inch is about the minimum for MIG spray-arc welding.

Equipment

MIG welder and power supply
Argon shielding gas
Wire/feed control
#4043 electrode wire
Cable and clamp assembly
Welding gun and cable assembly
Machine's owner's or service manual
Hand tools as needed
$1/4$-inch aluminum plate for welding

Safety Equipment

Welding gloves
Welding helmet
Steel-toed shoes

Task Completed

Procedure

1. Clean the weld area completely, both front and back, using wax and grease remover and a clean rag.   ❏

2. If the pieces to be welded are coated with a paint film, sand a strip about $3/4$ inch wide to the bare metal, using a disc sander and No. 80 disc. Do not press too hard, or the sander will heat up and peel off aluminum particles, clogging the paper.   ❏

3. Clean the metal until shiny with a stainless steel wire brush.   ❏

4. Load 0.030 aluminum wire into the welder and use 100 percent argon shielding gas. Trigger to extend the wire about $3/4$ to 1 inch beyond the nozzle.   ❏

5. Set the voltage, wire speed, and amount of argon gas, according to the instructions supplied with the welding machine. Remember that the wire speed must be faster than for steel. Set the tension of the wire drive roller lower to prevent twisting. But do not lower the tension too much or the wire speed will not be constant.   ❏

6. Nip off the end of the wire to remove the melt-down.   ❏

7. Position the two pieces of aluminum together.   ❏

8. Hold the gun closer to vertical when welding aluminum. Tilt it only about 5 to 15 degrees from the vertical in the direction of the weld.   ❏

9. Lay a bead along the entire joint. Use only the forward welding method (diagram below). Always push—never pull. When making a vertical weld, start at the bottom and work up.   ❑

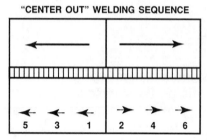 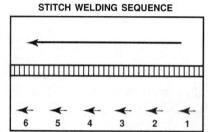

10. The distance between the contact tip and the weld should be $5/16$ to $9/16$ inch.   ❑

11. If the arc is too large, turn down the voltage and increase the wire speed. The bead should be uniform on top, with even penetration on the back.   ❑

Review Questions

Name_____ Date _____ Instructor Review _____

1. Technician A states that MIG welding is faster than stick welding. Technician B believes that MIG welding is easier to learn than stick welding. Who is correct?

    A. Technician A
    B. Technician B
    C. Both A and B
    D. Neither A nor B

2. Flux cored wire welding produces slag

    A. True
    B. False

3. DC reverse polarity means that the wire is

    _____.

4. A sputtering sound without any arc means that the voltage is too _____.

5. Technician A states that with the forehand method of MIG welding, the penetration depth is shallow. Technician B believes that with the backhand method, the bead is flat. Who is correct?

    A. Technician A
    B. Technician B
    C. Both A and B
    D. Neither A nor B

6. The gun angle for the forehand are backhand methods is ten to thirty degrees.

    A. True
    B. False

7. Technician A states that if the wire speed is set too slow, there will be spits and sputtering. Technician B believes that if the wire speed is too slow, there will be a much brighter reflected light. Who is correct?

    A. Technician A
    B. Technician B
    C. Both A and B
    D. Neither A nor B

8. Vertical welding is the technique of starting at the top and working your way downward.

    A. True
    B. False

9. When welding a butt joint, Technician A holds the gun at a 90 degree angle. Technician B holds the gun at a 30 degree angle. Who is correct?

    A. Technician A
    B. Technician B
    C. Both A and B
    D. Neither A nor B

10. Technician A makes a practice weld to test before he makes a structural weld. Technician B believes that a gun speed that is too slow will cause a melt through. Who is correct?

    A. Technician A
    B. Technician B
    C. Both A and B
    D. Neither A nor B

Job Sheet 8-1

Name_____ Date _____ Instructor Review _____

Buckle Exercise

Objective

After completing this lab, the student should be able to identify the different types of buckles.

Equipment

A car with parking lot dings or hail damage

Safety Equipment

Safety glasses

1.

Name of Buckle

1. _____

2. _____

3. _____

4. _____

5. _____

6. _____

7. _____

Indicate the Repair Sequence	Dolly Placement	Hammering Location
_____	_____	_____

2.

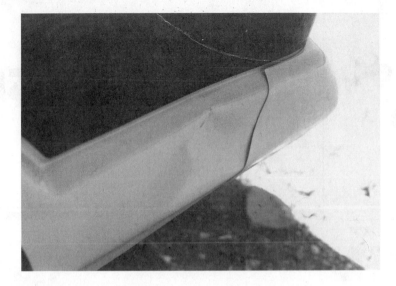

Name of Buckle Repair Method	Dolly Placement	Hammering Location

3.

Name of Buckle Repair Method	Dolly Placement	Hammering Location

4.

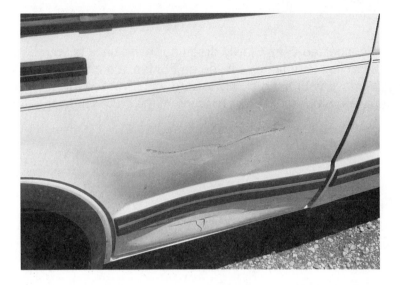

Name of Buckle Repair Method	Dolly Placement	Hammering Location

Locating Dents

Obtain a car with a few parking lot dings or hail damage. Wash the car if it is dirty and look at it in the shop. The dents are easier to see in dim light.

Sight

Look at the image of the overhead light in the car's paint surface. Any deviation from a straight line indicates a dent. Move your head from side to side as you sight the entire car, one panel at a time. The dents are much easier to see on a painted surface versus the ones found on a bare metal surface. Make a drawing of the car and indicate the dent locations. Compare your drawing with the other students.

Feel

Place your hand flat on a suspected dent. Slowly drag your hand back to your body. It is important to use your entire hand and not just your fingers. If you do not feel a dent, place a shop rag between your hand and the dent. Again, move your hand slowly toward you. Practice this technique until you feel comfortable with this detection process. Make a drawing of the car and indicate the location of the dents.

Job Sheet 8-2

Name_____ Date _____ Instructor Review _____

Metal Finishing

Objective

After completing this lab, the student should be able to metal finish simple buckles.

Equipment

Damaged fender
Metal file
Hammer and dolly

Safety Equipment

Safety glasses

Procedure

Task Completed

1. On a medium crown painted fender, make a dent with a dolly. ❑

2. Make a drawing of the dent. Indicate the repair sequence, hammer and dolly locations. ❑

3. Hammer and dolly the dent out following the written sequence. ❑

4. If the dent does not pop out, stop and rethink the sequence. ❑

5. Locate the highs and lows by feeling with your hand. ❑

6. Raise the lows and lower the highs by tapping hammer off dolly. ❑

7. Pick and file any remaining dents. ❑

8. Once this dent has been properly metal finished, make additional dents until you have completed six successful repairs. ❑

Job Sheet 8-3

Name_____ Date _____ Instructor Review _____

Tension Exercise

Objective

After completing this lab, the student should have an understanding of how heat and tension affect metal straightening.

Equipment

20 gauge sheet metal
Oxyacetylene torch
Ruler/tape measure
Hammer and dolly
Dozer
Ice or wet rag

Safety Equipment

Safety glasses

Procedure

Task Completed

1. Cut out four 4" x 12" pieces of 20 gauge sheet metal. Measure carefully. ❑

2. Heat one piece across the middle by rapidly passing a neutral flame over it. Heat until the metal is bright red. Allow it to air cool slowly. ❑

3. Heat another piece in the same manner as above. Rapidly cool it with a wet rag or ice. ❑

4. Bend another piece to demonstrate elastic deformation. Then bend it to show plastic deformation by pushing the ends together. ❑

5. Bend the remaining piece of sheet metal by pushing the ends together. Hammer the bend flat. ❑

6. Bend the air cooled and rapidly cooled pieces by pushing the ends together. ❑

7. Straighten all pieces with a hammer and dolly. ❑

8. Fill out this chart: ❑

Piece	Original Length	Repaired Length
A. Air cooled	_____	_____
B. Rapidly cooled	_____	_____
C. Bent	_____	_____
D. Hammered	_____	_____

Using molecular reasoning, explain the differences in length. _____

_____

_____

_____

9. Cut out six 4" x 14" pieces of sheet metal. Bend a 1" flange on both ends of each piece. Measure and record the lengths.   ❑

10. Bend three pieces by pushing the ends together (slightly bent). Bend three pieces by pushing the ends together. Then hammer the bend flat (badly bent).   ❑

11. Straighten one slightly bent and one badly bent piece by each of the following methods: ❑

   A. Tension and heat
   B. Tension and hammering
   C. Tension, heat and hammering

12. Fill out this chart: ❑

Tension & Heat	**Original Length**	**Repaired Length**
Slightly bent	_____	_____
Badly bent	_____	_____
Tension & Hammering		
Slightly bent	_____	_____
Badly bent	_____	_____
Tension, Heat & Hammering		
Slightly bent	_____	_____
Badly bent	_____	_____

Explain the reason for any difference between the original and repaired lengths. Which method is the most effective at restoring the original length? Why? _____

_____

_____

_____

_____

Job Sheet 8-4

Name_____ Date _____ Instructor Review _____

Stretch and Shrink Exercise

Objective

After completing this lab, the student should be able to properly stretch and shrink metal.

Equipment

Low crown panel
Oxyacetylene torch
Draw pin welder
Hammer and dolly
Shrinking hammer

Safety Equipment

Safety glasses
Dust respirator
Leather gloves

Procedure

Task Completed

1. Obtain a low crown panel. Remove the paint from an area at least 6" x 6" in size. ❑

2. Use a hammer on dolly to stretch the metal in an area no larger than 2" x 2". ❑

3. Review pages 257–259 in your textbook for the proper shrinking procedure. ❑

4. Use a torch, hammer and dolly to gradually shrink the stretched area. ❑

5. Once you have successfully completed this shrink, repeat until you have done this procedure correctly six times. ❑

6. Locate another area on the panel. Grind. Then slightly stretch the metal. ❑

7. Use a draw pin welder to shrink. If the draw pin welder has a shrinking attachment, then install it. If not, use the normal tip. Locate the highest spot of the stretch. Place the top of the draw pin welder at the highest spot. Push down and then press the trigger. Do not hold the trigger down. Continue around the stretched area until it matches the normal contour. ❑

8. Locate another suitable area and slightly stretch the metal. ❑

9. Use a shrinking hammer to bring down the high spot. A dolly can be used to support the adjacent metal. Utilize a light, rapid, spring hammering technique. Avoid hitting the dolly. ❑

10. Which method was the most effective at removing the stretch? Which method was the fastest? Which method required the most skill? _____ ❑

_____

_____

_____

_____

Job Sheet 8-5

Name_____ Date _____ Instructor Review _____

Paintless Dent Repair

Objective

After completing this lab, the student should be able to repair door dings without marring the paint surface.

Equipment

Paintless dent repair tools
Brick chisel
Car with door dings
Ball peen hammer

Safety Equipment

Safety glasses

Procedure

Task Completed

1. Obtain a car that has door dings or parking lot dents. Locate and mark the location of all the dents. ❏

2. Remove the interior trim as needed for access to the backside of the dented panel. If the damage is on the door or quarter panel, the disassembly might be quite extensive. If the dent is in the area of the door crash beam, backside access may be impossible. ❏

3. Once you've located an accessible dent, obtain a paintless dent repair rod that is long enough to reach and provide leverage. ❏

4. Watch for movement of the dent as you apply outward pressure. If the dent moves out, you are in the right place. ❏

5. Continue to apply outward pressure as you gradually move the face of the tool around the outside of the dent. Slowly work towards the center. ❏

6. Watch for movement of the dent. If there is no improvement, apply more outward pressure. Again, move in a circle, working from the outside to the inside. ❏

7. If no improvement is seen, use a leveraged back and forth movement across the dent. ❏

8. If the dent moves out and becomes a high spot, apply a piece of masking tape over the high area. Use the tool with thumb pressure on the taped area. Careful tapping will remove the dent. ❏

9. If there is a dent on a sharp body line, use a brick chisel on the back side of the line. Tap on the chisel as you look for movement. Careful tapping will remove the dent. ❏

10. Some dents may not be repairable. After you have successfully repaired one dent, continue until you have repaired twelve dents. ❏

Review Questions

Name_____ Date _____ Instructor Review _____

1. Hot-rolled sheet metal is used for unibodies.

   A. True
   B. False

2. The three types of high strength steel are

   _____,

   _____,

   and_____.

3. Technician A states that HSLA steel can be heated to 900 degree fahrenheit for three minutes with no loss in strength. Technician B believes that HSLA steel should not be oxyacetylene welded. Who is correct?

   A. Technician A
   B. Technician B
   C. Both A and B
   D. Neither A nor B

4. _____ is the bent shape metal takes after a collision.

5. _____ refers to a metal characteristic that allows it to spring back into shape after a force is released.

6. Technician A states that work hardening is put into panels to stiffen them. Technician B believes that work hardening is caused by deformation. Who is correct?

   A. Technician A
   B. Technician B
   C. Both A and B
   D. Neither A nor B

7. The two types of body damage are

   _____

   and_____.

8. The two types of hinge buckles are

   _____ and

   _____.

9. Technician A states that a collapsed rolled buckle tends to shrink the metal. Technician B believes that you should use a hammer on dolly to correct the shrinkage. Who is correct?

   A. Technician A
   B. Technician B
   C. Both A and B
   D. Neither A nor B

10. Last in, first out.

    A. True
    B. False

Chapter 9

Minor Auto Body Repairs

Job Sheet 9-1

Name_____ Date _____ Instructor Review _____

Hail Dents

Objective

After completing this lab, the student should be able to repair hail dents.

Equipment

Low crown panel
Microtorch
Ball peen hammer
Hammer and dolly
Metal file
Straight edge

Safety Equipment

Safety glasses
Dust respirator
Leather gloves

Procedure

Task Completed

1. This repair method is meant to simulate a repair to a hail damaged roof. This is a one-sided repair because in most cases, the car's headliner would not be removed. Only the outside of the roof would be worked. ❏

2. Obtain a hail damaged low crown panel. If a damaged panel is not available, then use a deck lid, roof or hood. Use a ball peen hammer to create ten small dents. ❏

3. Use a butane powere micro torch to heat a circle around the outside of the dent. Watch for movement in the panel. If the heated area moves down, stop and let it air cool. Start further out from the center of the dent and gradually work toward the center. Continually watch for movement. ❏

4. When the heated dented area moves above the level of the surrounding metal, remove the heat. Quickly file down the heated high spot. ❏

5. Do not quench with water. Allow the panel to air cool. ❏

**Task
Completed**

6. Low spots can be identified as areas with burnt paint. High spots show deep file marks.   ❏

7. If high areas remain after filing, use a sharp pick hammer to level them. Hit on the high, ridged areas only.   ❏

8. Remaining low areas must be filled. It is not advisable to heat the spots excessively.   ❏

9. Check the repair by hand and with a straight edge.   ❏

10. When you have completed one repair properly, repeat this procedure until you have successfully repaired twelve dents.   ❏

Job Sheet 9-2

Name_____ Date _____ Instructor Review _____

Body Filler Exercise

Objective

After completing this lab, the student should be able to properly mix, apply, and finish body filler.

Equipment

Fender
Metal file
Cheese grater
Grinder
Ball peen hammer/pick hammer
Straight edge
Long board
40, 80, 220 grit paper

Safety Equipment

Safety glasses
Dust respirator
Leather gloves

Procedure

Task Completed

1. Obtain a medium crown panel, such as the upper portion of a fender. Do not use a low crown panel like a hood or deck lid for this exercise. ❑

2. Grind the paint off in an area of about 4" x 12". ❑

3. Use a ball peen hammer to make at least twenty small dents in the bare metal area. ❑

4. Lay a straight edge on the bare metal area. High spots are evident if the straight edge rocks. Identify and remove the high areas by pick hammering. If any high spots remain after the body filler application, they will show up in the sanding. ❑

5. Mix the body filler following the directions on page 274–277 in your textbook. ❑

6. Do not apply any body filler over paint. If you do have a dent near the paint edge, then grind the paint back two inches. ❑

7. Put the body filler on the bare metal area with a hard downward pressure on the first coat. Overfill the dent. Do not excessively work the area. ❑

8. When the body filler has cured to the hardness of processed cheese, use a cheese grater to quickly remove the excess filler. If the body filler rolls off the bare metal, then it has not cured enough. Allow additional cure time. ❑

9. When the body filler has been cheese-grated and has dried into a hard surface, it can be sanded with a long board and 40 grit paper. The long board should cover the entire repair area. As you sand, keep the ends of the long board on the undamaged areas. This will allow you to match the contour of the panel. ❑

10. When the body filler is almost completely sanded, switch to 80 grit paper on the long board. Use the 80 grit paper to remove the deep scratches made by the 40 grit paper. ❑

**Task
Completed**

11. Check the sanded area with your hand. The body filler must be smooth. There
     should be no lumps or dips. Have your instructor feel the repair.   ❑

12. Your goal is to do metal work, fill once and finish. If your repair had problems,
     repeat the exercise until you can finish with one filler application.   ❑

Job Sheet 9-3

Name_____ Date _____ Instructor Review _____

One-Sided Repair

Objective

After completing this lab, the student should be able to make a one-sided repair on a vehicle.

Equipment

Damaged vehicle
Draw pins
Slide hammer
Metal file
40 grit paper
Draw pin welder
Pick hammer
Body filler
Long board

Safety Equipment

Safety glasses
Dust respirator
Leather gloves

Procedure

Task Completed

1. This repair will be made on the outside only. An example of this type of repair would be a door dent. See page 256 in your textbook for an example. Obtain this type of damaged panel.   ❑

2. Identify the high ridges and low areas. Make an outline drawing of the damage.   ❑

3. Plan the repair sequence. Indicate on your drawing where draw pins will be welded and ridges will be hammered.   ❑

4. Grind the paint from the low areas. Your instructor will demonstrate how to operate the draw pin welder. Follow the plan and weld on the draw pins.   ❏

5. Use the slide hammer to gradually raise the low area. Start in the center. Work the low spot up slightly. Switch to another draw pin. Pull out on the slide hammer as you spring hammer the ridges. Gradually work the center of the dent.   ❏

6. When you have pulled on all of the pins, begin at the edges. Pull them out until they are level. Continue hammering any remaining ridges.   ❏

7. Check the panel with a straight edge and by hand. Identify and high spots.   ❏

8. If high spots are found, support the metal by pulling out on the draw pin with the slide hammer. With the panel supported, hammer on the high spot. If it does not move, use a sharp pick hammer to shrink it. Start at the highest point and work outward.   ❏

9. Again check the panel for high and low spots. Low spots less than one-eighth inch can be filled. Any low spot deeper than one-eighth inch must be raised with a draw pin. If you over-pull, use a sharp pick hammer to shrink the spot. If the draw pin breaks off and forms a hole in the panel, you must weld the hole shut.   ❏

10. Check the panel by hand to locate any remaining high spots. When there are no remaining high spots, you can begin the application of body filler.   ❏

11. Mix, apply, sand, and finish sand the body filler as you did in Job Sheet #9-2. If bare metal shows up while you are sanding the body filler, you have discovered a high spot. Pick this spot down. If this area is low after picking, then refill.   ❏

12. The two most common mistakes are applying body filler before all of the high spots are removed and not putting in an overfill of body filler. Avoid these problems by carefully checking the panel for high spots and completely filling the low areas. If you have encountered one or both of these problems, repeat the exercise until you accomplish it correctly.   ❏

Job Sheet 9-4

Name_____ Date _____ Instructor Review _____

Tension Panel Repair

Objective

After completing this lab, the student should be able to repair a quarter panel dent with tension.

Equipment

Damaged quarter panel
Four ton porto power
Metal file
Hammer and dolly
Straight edge
Oxyacetylene torch
Draw pin welder

Safety Equipment

Safety glasses
Dust respirator
Leather gloves

Procedure

Task Completed

1. Obtain a quarter panel with a severe dent. This dent must change the length of the panel. Note any improper gaps between the deck lid and the quarter panel, tail light and quarter panel, or rear bumper and the quarter panel.   ❏

2. Draw a diagram of the repair. Indicate the buckles and the porto power push directions. Write out a plan of repair. Indicate which buckles will be removed first.   ❏

_____
_____
_____
_____
_____
_____
_____
_____

Task Completed

3. Set up a four ton porto power inside the trunk. Set the ram against a bracket on the inner wheel house. If this is not stable, brace an area inside the trunk with pieces of 2" x 4" boards. Monitor this base during the push operation. If there is distortion, stop and rebrace.   ❏

4. Add extension tubes to the ram to reach the inner corner at the rear of the quarter panel. Install the appropriate head on the tube.   ❏

5. Begin pushing operations by closing the ram value and pumping the jack. Watch for movement in the lowest area of the dent. Apply only a small amount of tension on the dent.   ❏

6. Follow the repair plan with hammer and dolly, releasing the buckles in the prescribed sequence. Apply additional tension with the ram. Do not overextend the panel.   ❏

7. Check for proper gaps. When the gaps line up, overextend slightly to allow for spring back.   ❏

8. Work any remaining high and low spots with hammer and dolly.   ❏

9. An area that pushes in and pops out is called an "oil can." This can be repaired by shrinking. Use the draw pin welder in small areas (the size of a quarter) and a torch on larger areas. All "oil cans" must be removed before you can apply body filler.   ❏

10. Check the panel for high areas by hand and with a straight edge. If no high areas are found and all low areas are less than $1/8$" deep, grind off the paint. Apply body filler, sand, guide coat and proof sand.   ❏

Job Sheet 9-5

Name_____ Date _____ Instructor Review _____

Hood Repair

Objective

After completing this lab, the student should be able to repair a damaged hood.

Equipment

A damaged hood
Hammer and dolly
Wood block
DA
Spoon
Body filler
Draw pin welder
Metal file

Safety Equipment

Safety glasses
Dust respirator
Leather gloves

Procedure

Task Completed

1. Obtain a hood that has been hit in the front with a resulting buckle near the middle of the length of the hood. This type of damage raises the hood buckle above the level of the fender. ❑

2. Make a drawing of the damage and plan out the repair sequence. ❑

_____

_____

_____

_____

_____

_____

_____

**Task
Completed**

3. Place a wood block under the front edge of the hood. This will give the hood room to flex. ❏

4. Use a dinging spoon and a ball peen hammer on the ridge. Hold the spoon tightly and rapidly hammer on it. If the ridge does not move, use a 2" x 4" board set on edge in place of the spoon. Remove the block of wood and check the hood for level against the fender. If the ridge is not level with the fender, continue "spooning" the ridge. If access is available under the hood, the hammer and dolly can be used. ❏

5. Many hoods have a body line to stiffen the panel. A brick chisel can be used to lower the ridge on the body line. The chisel end of a hammer may also be used. ❏

6. Remove the pain four inches on either side with 80 grit paper on a dual-action sander. Do not use a grinder. It will produce too much heat and warp the metal. ❏

7. The metal around the ridge is softer than the ridge itself. Use a shrink fence to prevent this soft area from rising up during finishing. A shrink fence can be made by surrounding the ridge with a series of pin shrinks. Use the draw pin welder to tighten the metal adjacent to the ridge. Lightly tap the trigger of the welder to create the smallest amount of heat. Place a higher concentration of pin shrinks near near the ridge. Fewer shrinks are placed further away from the ridge. (See the diagram below.) An alternative shrink fence method is to use a sharp pick hammer instead of welds. ❏

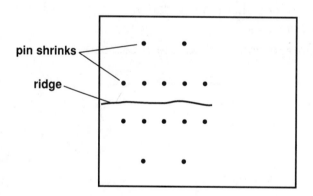

8. Check the panel for high and low areas with a straight edge and by hand. Remove the high areas with a draw pin welder, pick hammer or shrinking hammer. ❏

9. When all of the high areas are removed and all low areas are less than $1/8$" deep with the panel tight, apply body filler. Sand the panel carefully as hoods are easily distorted with excessive heat. ❏

Review Questions

Name_____ Date _____ Instructor Review _____

1. Technician A adds extra hardener to body filler for a fast cure. Technician B puts body filler over the paint. Who is correct?

   A. Technician A
   B. Technician B
   C. Both A and B
   D. Neither A nor B

2. You must always metal etch bare metal before you apply body filler.

   A. True
   B. False

3. Technician A uses waterproof body filler to fill holes in metal. Technician B uses regular body filler to fill holes in metal. Who is correct?

   A. Technician A
   B. Technician B
   C. Both A and B
   D. Neither A nor B

4. Technician A fills pin holes with one part glazing putty. Technician B fills pin holes with two part glazing putty. Who is correct?

   A. Technician A
   B. Technician B
   C. Both A and B
   D. Neither A nor B

5. You should use a stick to mix the body filler and a spreader to apply it.

   A. True
   B. False

6. Technician A mixes body filler on a piece of sheet metal. Technician B uses a plastic board of mix body filler. Who is correct?

   A. Technician A
   B. Technician B
   C. Both A and B
   D. Neither A nor B

7. Technician A uses a cheese grater to level semi-cured body filler. Technician B waits for the body filler to harden completely; then he sands it. Who is correct?

   A. Technician A
   B. Technician B
   C. Both A and B
   D. Neither A nor B

8. Technician A states that filling rust-outs with waterproof body filler is an acceptable repair. Technician B believes that any rust repair is a temporary fix. Who is correct?

   A. Technician A
   B. Technician B
   C. Both A and B
   D. Neither A nor B

9. Technician A states that lead is the only way to properly fill a dent. Technician B believes that when used properly, body filler is as good as lead. Who is correct?

   A. Technician A
   B. Technician B
   C. Both A and B
   D. Neither A nor B

10. A body filler thickness of $1/4$" or less is acceptable.

    A. True
    B. False

Chapter 10
Diagnosing Major Collision Damage

Shop Assignment 10-1

Name_____ Date _____ Instructor Review _____

Measurement Introduction

Measurements

1. Measure hole diameter

mm _____
inches _____

mm _____
inches _____

mm _____
inches _____

2. Measure hole center
    Diameter/2

mm   _____

inches   _____

mm   _____

inches   _____

mm   _____

inches   _____

3. Measure center to center distance

mm   _____

inches   _____

mm   _____

inches   _____

mm   _____

inches   _____

mm   _____

inches   _____

mm   _____

inches   _____

mm   _____

inches   _____

Notice that when measuring center to center on the same size holes, you can get the same result by measuring the near side of one hole to the far side of the other hole.

4. X check hole to hole

1   2   1-4   mm   _____

                                                    inches _____

3   4   2-3   mm   _____

                                                    inches _____

Shop Assignment 10-2

Name_____ Date _____ Instructor Review _____

Simulated Vehicle Measurements

1. X check engine compartment

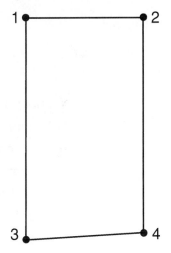

1-4	mm	_____
	inches	_____
2-3	mm	_____
	inches	_____

2. Under hood measurements

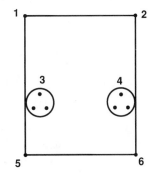

Length

1-5 mm _____
     inches _____
2-6 mm _____
     inches _____

Width

1-2 mm _____
     inches _____
3-4 mm _____
     inches _____
5-6 mm _____
     inches _____

X checks

1-4 mm _____
     inches _____
2-3 mm _____
     inches _____
3-6 mm _____
     inches _____
4-5 mm _____
     inches _____
1-6 mm _____
     inches _____
2-5 mm _____
     inches _____

3.   Radius measurement

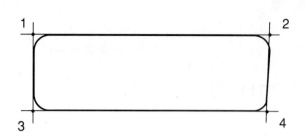

X checks

1-4   mm   _____

     inches   _____

2-3   mm   _____

     inches   _____

Draw straight lines to form a point, measure point to point.

4.   Underbody measurements
    Full frame pick truck

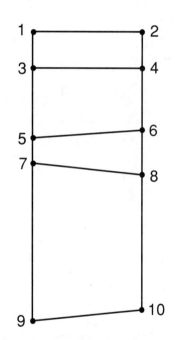

X checks

1-6   mm   _____

     inches   _____

2-5   mm   _____

     inches   _____

1-4   mm   _____

     inches   _____

2-3   mm   _____

     inches   _____

5-8   mm   _____

     inches   _____

6-7   mm   _____

     inches   _____

7-10 mm   _____

     inches   _____

8-9   mm   _____

     inches   _____

5.   Upper body measurements
    Door opening

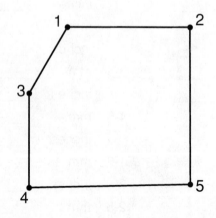

X checks

1-5   mm   _____

     inches   _____

3-5   mm   _____

     inches   _____

2-4   mm   _____

     inches   _____

Deck lid opening

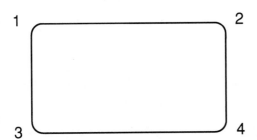

X checks

1-4   mm   _____

      inches   _____

2-3   mm   _____

      inches   _____

Windshield opening

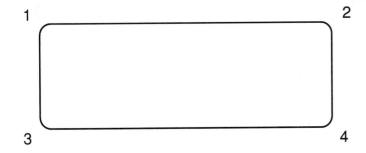

X checks

1-4   mm   _____

      inches   _____

2-3   mm   _____

      inches   _____

Shop Assignment 10-3

Name_____ Date _____ Instructor Review _____

Misalignment Measurements

1. Write in these measurements:

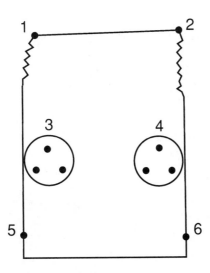

Width

1-2 _____

3-4 _____

7-8 _____

X checks

1-6 _____

2-5 _____

1-8 _____

2-7 _____

What types of damage conditions? _____

_____

_____

2.

Width

1-2 _____

5-6 _____

X checks

1-4 _____

2-3 _____

1-6 _____

2-5 _____

What types of damage conditions? _____

_____

_____

3.

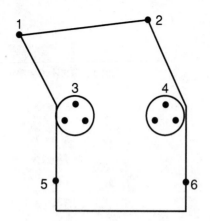

Width

1-2   _____

5-6   _____

X checks

1-4   _____

2-3   _____

1-6   _____

2-5   _____

What types of damage conditions? _____

_____

_____

Shop Assignment 10-4

Name_____ Date _____ Instructor Review _____

Frame Manual

Bottom View

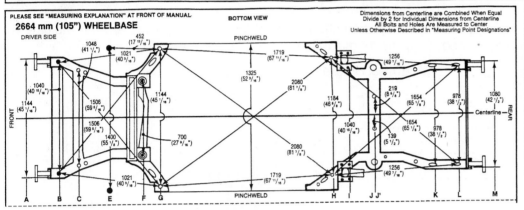

1. Is the engine cradle X check symmetrical or asymmetrical? _____

2. What is the measurement used for the X check of the vehicle center section? _____

3. What is the vehicle width between the pinch welds? _____

4. What is the width between the rear bolts of the engine cradle? _____

5. What is the width between the rear bumper bracket outer lower bolts? _____

6. What is the wheelbase dimension?_____

Side View

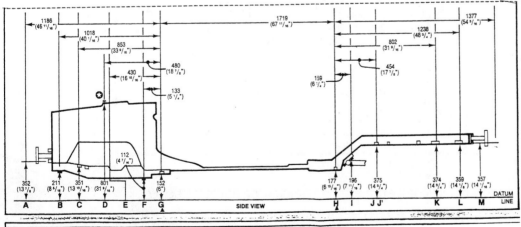

1. What is the total vehicle length? _____

2. What is the datum height of the engine cradle front bolt? _____

3. What is the datum height of the rear suspension mount rear bolt?_____

4. What is the distance between the rear suspension mount, rear bolt and the oval hole at the rear of the frame? You need to hang gauges and set datum on this car. Fill out this chart.

Gauge #	Letter	Type of Hole	Height
1	_____	_____	_____
2	_____	_____	_____
3	_____	_____	_____
4	_____	_____	_____

You find that due to the exhaust system clearance, you must lower a guage by 50 mm. Indicate the distance between the unibody and the frame gauge.

Gauge #	Modified Height
1	_____
2	_____
3	_____
4	_____

Engine Compartment

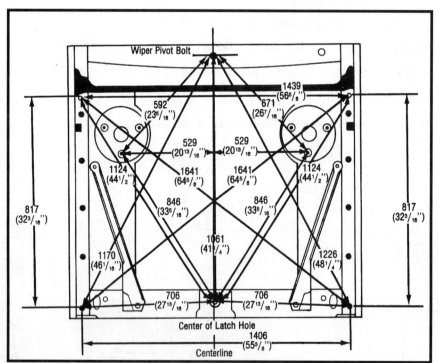

1. Is the X check of the engine compartment symmetrical or asymmetrical? _____

2. What is the X check of the engine compartment?_____

3. What is the width of the radiator support? _____

4. What is the distance between the front shock tower and the center of the latch hole?

   _____

5. What is the width between the front bolts of the shock towers? _____

Truck

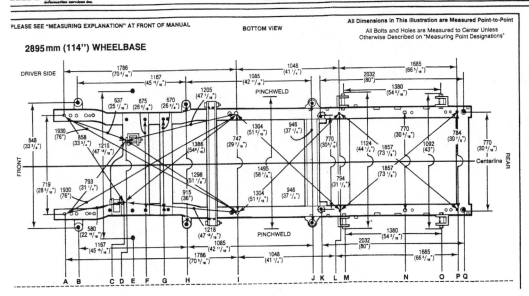

Underview

1. What is the wheel base? _____

2. What is the width between the pinch welds? _____

3. What bolts are used to X check under the bed? _____

4. What is the distance between the spring pivot bolts? _____

5. What is the width at the radiator support mounts? _____

6. What is the width at the rear cab mounts? _____

Side

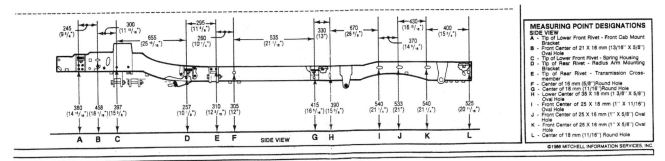

1. What is the datum height at the transmission cross member? _____

2. What is the datum height at the radius arm mounting bracket? _____

3. What is the datum distance between the radiator support? _____

4. What is the datum height at the rear of the frame? _____

You need to hang gauges and set datum on this vehicle.

Gauge	Letter	Type of Hole	Height
1	_____	_____	_____
2	_____	_____	_____
3	_____	_____	_____
4	_____	_____	_____

You need to lower the gauges by 75 mm. Indicate the distance between the gauge and the frame.

Gauge	Modified Height
1	_____
2	_____
3	_____
4	_____

Underhood

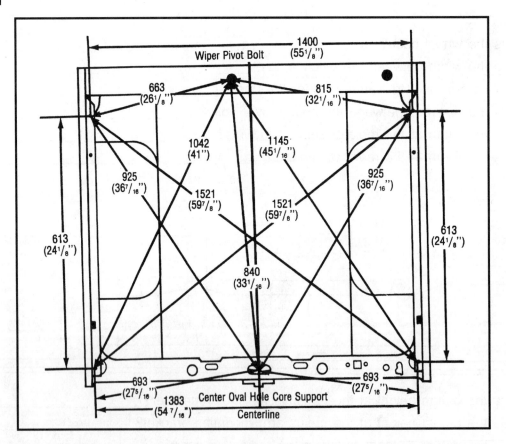

1. Is the engine compartment X check symmetrical?_____
2. What is the engine compartment X check? _____
3. What is the width at the radiator support? _____

Shop Assignment 10-5

Name_____ Date _____ Instructor Review _____

Vehicle Damage

1.

A. Where was the point of impact? _____

_____

_____

B. List the damaged body parts._____

_____

_____

C. List the likely frame damage conditions. _____

_____

_____

D. How can you determine cowl damage from this picture? _____

_____

_____

2.

A. Where was the point of impact? _____

_____

_____

B. List the damaged body parts. _____

_____

_____

C. List the likely frame damage conditions. _____

_____

_____

3.

A. Where was the point of impact? _____

_____

_____

B. List the damaged body parts._____

_____

_____

C. List the damaged suspension and steering parts. _____

_____

_____

D. List the damaged suspension and steering parts. _____

_____

_____

4.

A. Where was the point of impact? _____

_____

_____

B. List the damaged body parts. _____

_____

_____

C. List the likely frame damage conditions. _____

_____

_____

Shop Assignment 10-6

Name_____ Date _____ Instructor Review _____

Gauge Reading

Answer questions A and B for each diagram shown:

1.

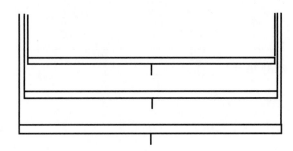

   A. Is there a problem?_____

   B. If there is a problem, what is it? _____

   _____

   _____

2.

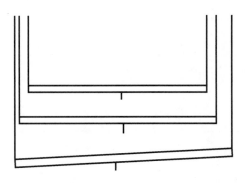

   A. Is there a problem?_____

   B. If there is a problem, what is it? _____

   _____

   _____

3.

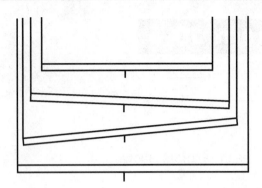

A. Is there a problem?_____

B. If there is a problem, what is it? _____

_____

_____

4.

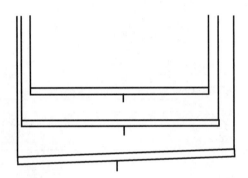

A. Is there a problem?_____

B. If there is a problem, what is it? _____

_____

_____

Shop Assignment 10-7

Name_____ Date _____ Instructor Review _____

Damage Diagrams

Damage diagrams should be made whenever a frame damaged vehicle is repaired. You will save repair time if you diagram the damage and plan out the pulls needed to square the vehicle.

1. Unibody—Upper View
   Make an outline drawing of the vehicle. This is similar to what you see in frame dimension manuals. It does not have to be overly detailed. Include the engine compartment and indicate the location of the gauges. Write in any damage conditions such as sidesway and mash. Here is an example.

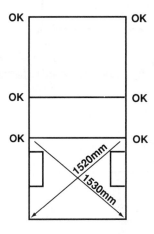

2. Unibody—Side View
   Again, make a drawing of the vehicle. This view will describe datum problems and indicate roof damage and mash. Here is an example.

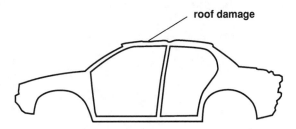

roof damage

3. Pickup Truck—Upper View
   An outline drawing is made of the pickup frame. Damage is indicated by labeling at the control points, such as twist, diamond, mash, and sidesway. (See below.)

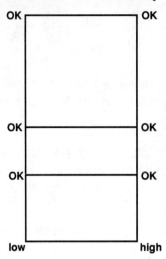

4. Pickup Truck—Side View
   Make a side view of the frame. Indicate sag or mash damage.

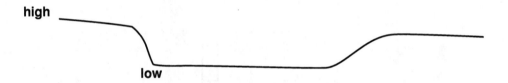

Make damage diagrams based on these descriptions.

1. Unibody car hit in the right front. Gauges 2, 3, 4 are all level to each other. Gauge 1 is low on the right side. X check of the front fender bolts to the shock tower is:

   Left fender to right shock tower 110 mm.
   Right fender to left shock tower 98 mm.
   Center line is fine.

2. Unibody Car. Gauges 2, 3, and 4 are level to each other. Gauge 1 is high on the right, low on the left. X check of the front fender bolts to the shock tower is:

    Left fender to the right shock tower 125 mm.
    Right fender to the left shock tower 107 mm.
    Center line is off to the left by 5 mm.

3. Pickup Truck. Gauges 1, 2, 3, and 4 are level. X check under the cab is off by 10 mm. Center line is fine.

4. Pickup Truck. Gauges 3 and 4 are level to each other. Gauge 2 is high on the left and low on the right. Gauge 1 is high on the right and low on the left. X check under the cab is off by 2 mm. Center line shows that gauge 1 is off of center by 7 mm.

Job Sheet 10-1

Name_____ Date _____ Instructor Review _____

Unibody Measurements

Objective

After completing this lab, the student should be able to make measurements on cars and compare them to a reference.

Equipment

Undamaged unibody car
Tape measure
Frame dimension guide
Tram

Safety Equipment

Safety glasses

Procedure

	Actual	Reference
1. Use a tram to X check the engine compartment. Consult the guide for points to measure.	_____	_____
2. Use a tram to measure a door opening. Use the reference measurement points.	_____	_____
3. Use the tram to measure the windshield opening. Use reference measurement points.	_____	_____

Obtain a different undamaged unibody car. Fill out the following chart:

Measurement	Value
Rear bolt, left fender—front bolt, right fender	_____
Rear bolt, right fender—front bolt, right fender	_____
Left shock tower—center of hood latch hole	_____
Right shock tower—center of hood latch hole	_____
Width between the shock towers	_____
Width between the fenders at the front	_____
Width between the fenders at the rear	_____

Make a line drawing of the engine compartment. Indicate all of the distances.

Make measurements of a door opening. Fill out this chart:

Measurement Points	**Value**
_____	_____
_____	_____
_____	_____

Make a line drawing of the door opening. Indicate all of the distances.

Job Sheet 10-2

Name_____ Date _____ Instructor Review _____

Damaged Vehicle Measurements

Objective

After completing this lab, the student should be able to make measurements on a damaged vehicle.

Equipment

Damaged unibody car
Tape measure
Tram gauge

Safety Equipment

Safety glasses

Procedure

Obtain a damaged unibody car. Walk around the car and note all of the damage.

List the improper gaps on this chart:

Panel Gaps	Problem
_____	_____
_____	_____
_____	_____

List the damaged outer panels on this chart:

Panels	Problem
_____	_____
_____	_____
_____	_____

Lift the hood. Fill out the chart and make a line drawing of the opening. Indicate the measurements.

Panels	**Problem**
_____	_____
_____	_____
_____	_____

Measure all door openings. Make a drawing indicating the distances.

Job Sheet 10-3

Name_____ Date _____ Instructor Review _____

Quick Checks

Objective

After completing this lab, the student should be able to make quick checks for damage to vehicles.

Equipment

Front-end hit unibody car
Car with rear wheel wobble
Wrench
Masking tape
Socket and rachet

Safety Equipment

Safety glasses

Procedure

Steering Arm and Steering Gear Damage Checks   **Task Completed**

1. Turn the steering wheel from lock to lock.   ❑

2. Count the number of turns when you turn it again from lock to lock.   ❑

3. Multiply the number of turns by one-half. The result will be used in step 4.   ❑

4. Using the result in step three, turn the steering wheel that number of times.   ❑

5. Place masking tape at the top center of the wheel.   ❑
    Check to see which condition exists:

    A. If the steering wheel is centered and the wheels point straight ahead, there isn't any problem.

    B. If the steering wheel is centered but the wheels do not point straight ahead, there could be steering arm damage.

    C. If the steering wheel is off center and the wheels point straight ahead, there could be steering gear damage.

Bump Steer Check

1. Center and mark the steering wheel as in the previous check.   ❑

2. Bounce the front of the vehicle up and down.   ❑
    If the steering wheel turns during the bouncing, the rack and pinion may be out-of-level.

Bent Strut Check

1. Move the strut lock nut one-half to one turn.   ❑

2. Turn the strut shaft.   ❑

3. Look at the wheel as you turn the shaft. Any change in camber indicates a bent strut.   ❑

4. Torque the lock nut to specifications.   ❑

**Task
Completed**

Strut Location

1. Jack up the vehicle and place the jack stands. ❑

2. Remove the front wheels. ❑

3. Use a straight edge to measure the distance from strut to rotor on both sides of the vehicle. ❑

4. Compare the measurements. Any differences indicate a bent strut, bent rotor or damaged steering knuckle. ❑

Rear Wheel Wobble

1. Jack up the rear of the car and place it on jack stands. ❑

2. Place a pencil on a jack stand. Position the pencil to within $\frac{1}{8}$" of the wheel. ❑

3. Spin the wheel. Look at the distance between the wheel and the pencil as the wheel spins. Any change in distance indicates a bent wheel or axle. ❑

4. If there is a change in distance, remove the wheel. ❑

5. Replace the pencil. Position it near the rear brake drum. ❑

6. Spin the drum. Any difference in distance between the drum and the pencil indicates a bent axle. ❑

Job Sheet 10-4

Name_____ Date _____ Instructor Review _____

Hanging Frame Gauges

Objective

After completing this lab, the student should be able to hang gauges on unibody and frame vehicles.

Equipment

Unibody car, truck
Frame gauges
Tram

Safety Equipment

Safety glasses

Procedure

Obtain an undamaged pickup truck.

Task Completed

Diamond

1. Use a tram gauge or a steel tape to check for diamond under the cab. Make an X check under the cab. Do not use the cab mount bolts, as they are easily bent in an accident, giving a false reading. Find two sets of rivets or holes that are on the same place on either frame rail. X check these. Any difference greater than $1/4$" or 6 mm indicates diamond damage.   ❑

Twist

2. Next check for level under the cab. Consult a frame dimension guide for holes to hange the gauges. Set the height of each gauge according to specifications. Install the center line pins. Sight the gauges. Stand at least ten feet away from the truck. Use both eyes to sight the gauges. If the gauges are not parallel, twist damage is present.   ❑

Level

3. Now check for level by hanging a gauge with center line pins at the front of the truck and another gauge at the rear of the truck. Use the guide to determine the location and the height. Read the front gauge into the base gauge. If the front or rear gauges are not parallel to the base gauges, an out-of-level condition exists.   ❑

Center Line

4. Stand at least ten feet away from the truck and sight the center line pins with one eye. If this is difficult, stretch a piece of string alongside the pins. Any deviation greater than $1/8$" or 3 mm indicates sidesway.   ❑

5. Recheck the gauges to be sure that they are at the specified height. Sight the front and rear gauges into the base gauges. All gauges should be at the same height. Any difference in height indicates a datum misalignment.   ❑

Obtain an undamaged unibody car. Use the same procedures as the truck, except start at number 2 because diamond damage is not expected in a unibody.

Twist   _____

Level   _____

Center line   _____

Datum   _____

If your gauge set includes a strut tower measuring bridge, set it up and check for the center line.

Strut tower   _____

Job Sheet 10-5

Name_____ Date _____ Instructor Review _____

Evaluate Damaged Unibody

Objective

After completing this lab, the student should be able to evaluate a damaged unibody vehicle.

Equipment

Damaged unibody
Frame gauges
Tram

Safety Equipment

Safety glasses

Procedure

1. Walk around the vehicle. Check the door, fender, hood and deck lid gaps. Record any deviations. _____

   _____

   _____

2. Open the hood and X check. X check the doors and deck lid openings.

	X Check Values	Problem
Hood	_____	_____
Door	_____	_____
Door	_____	_____
Door	_____	_____
Door	_____	_____
Deck Lid	_____	_____

3. Hang gauges using the proper sequence. Twist. Level. Center Line. Datum.

	Problem
Twist	_____
Level	_____
Center Line	_____
Datum	_____

4. Draw a damage diagram. Indicate all damage on this vehicle.

Job Sheet 10-6

Name_____ Date _____ Instructor Review _____

Evaluate Damaged Truck

Objective

After completing this lab, the student should be able to diagnose and fill out a damage sheet on a truck.

Equipment

Truck with frame damage
Tram gauge
Self-centering gauges

Safety Equipment

Safety glasses

Procedure

Task Completed

1. Walk around the truck. What was the point of impact? Sight the tailgate into the rear window. Is it level? Sight the bed and cab gap. Is it even? ❏

2. Your instructor will show you where to place the floor jack to raise the truck. Place the jack stands where they will not interfere with the gauges. ❏

3. Consult a frame dimension guide for locations to measure diamond and where to hang gauges. ❏

4. Check for diamond by using the tram gauge under the cab. Do not use the cab mount bolts. X check rivets or holes under the cab. Any difference greater than one-fourth of an inch in the X check indicates diamond damage. Record this result on the sheet. ❏

5. Check for twist by handing a gauge under the cowl and under the rear of the cab. Consult the guide for proper height. Move at least ten feet away from the truck and use both eyes to sight the gauges. Any difference in height indicates twist. Record the result. ❏

6. Hang a gauge in the area of the radiator support. Set it at the the proper height. Read this gauge into the one at the cowl. Any difference in height indicated out of level. Record the result. ❏

7. Hang the gauge at the correct height at the rear of the truck. Sight this gauge into the one at the rear of the cab. Record the result. ❏

8. Set the center line pins in the gauges. Sight all gauges by standing ten feet back and using one eye. A string can be placed alongside the pins as a guide. If out of level and sidesway is indicated, move the low side of the out of level gauge up until it is level. Now check for sidesway. If the sidesway is gone, this is known as a pendulum effect, i.e., an out of level gauge that looks like a sidesway. Record the results. ❏

9. Check for datum. Sight across the top of all the gauges. Record the results. ❏

10. Make the measurements. Measure from a uniform hole on both sides of the frame to each lower ball joint. Record the results.

11. Make a damage diagram of the vehicle. Indicate all damage.

Review Questions

Name_____ Date _____ Instructor Review _____

1. Technician A states that if a car hits a tree, the damage will not be as bad as the damage from hitting a brick wall. Technician B believes that a wall will cause less damage than a tree. Who is correct?

   A. Technician A
   B. Technician B
   C. Both A and B
   D. Neither A nor B

2. Technician A states that sag is the most common type of collision damage. Technician B believes that sidesway is the most common type of collision damage. Who is right?

   A. Technician A
   B. Technician B
   C. Both A and B
   D. Neither A nor B

3. Technician A states that diamond occurs only in full frame vehicles. Technician B believes that twisting rarely occurs in unibody vehicles. Who is correct?

   A. Technician A
   B. Technician B
   C. Both A and B
   D. Neither A nor B

4. When looking for damage, Technician A checks for cracked paint. Technician B checks for cracked undercoat. Who is correct?

   A. Technician A
   B. Technician B
   C. Both A and B
   D. Neither A nor B

5. To check for inertia damage on a pickup truck, look for an out-of-parallel condition between the _____

   and the _____.

6. When measuring a damaged car, Technician A consults a frame dimension manual. Technician B takes measurements from the same type of vehicle. Who is correct?

   A. Technician A
   B. Technician B
   C. Both A and B
   D. Neither A nor B

7. When measuring point to point, Technician A uses a tram gauge. For the same situation, Technician B uses a steel tape measure. Who is correct?

   A. Technician A
   B. Technician B
   C. Both A and B
   D. Neither A nor B

8. An undamaged car is _____ if the measurements on the right side of the vehicle do not match the measurements on the left side.

9. Technician A hangs two gauges to check for center line. Technician B hangs three gauges to check for center line. Who is correct?

   A. Technician A
   B. Technician B
   C. Both A and B
   D. Neither A nor B

10. Technician A states that a universal bench is needed to measure a severely damaged unibody. Technician B believes that a laser system gives a better measurement. Who is correct?

    A. Technician A
    B. Technician B
    C. Both A and B
    D. Neither A nor B

Chapter 11

Body Alignment

Shop Assignment 11-1

Name_____ Date _____ Instructor Review _____

Pull Plans

In this example, the center section and right side need to be held in place. The left corner needs to be moved sideways and down.

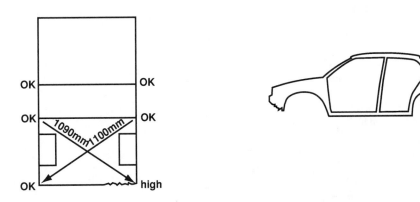

This drawing indicates the hookups and tie downs needed to repair this vehicle.

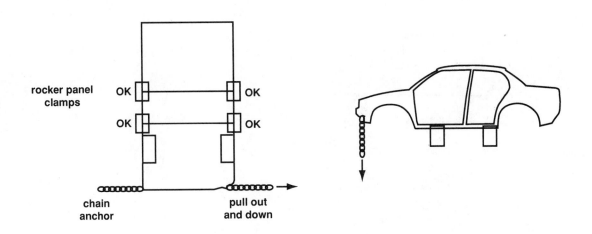

Draw in the hookups and tie down on the following damage diagrams.

1.

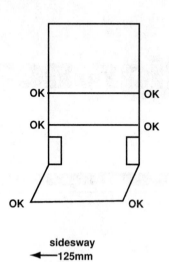

sidesway
←125mm

2.

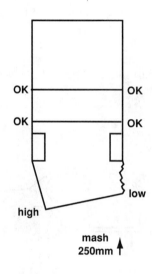

mash
250mm ↑

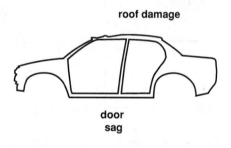

roof damage

door
sag

3.

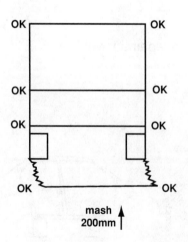

mash
200mm ↑

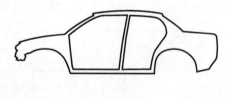

4.

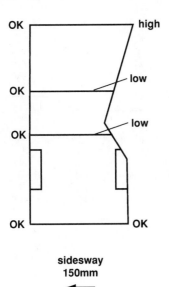

sidesway
150mm

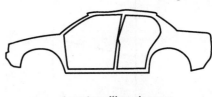

roof damage

center pillow damage
rocker panel damage

5.

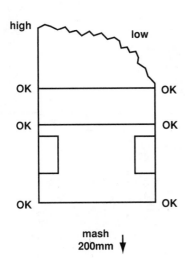

mash
200mm

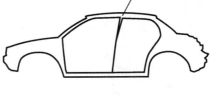

improper door gap

6.

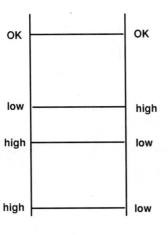

twist

7.

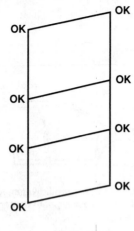

diamond

8.

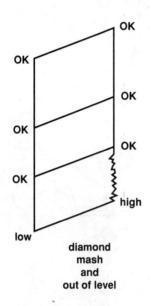

diamond
mash
and
out of level

9.

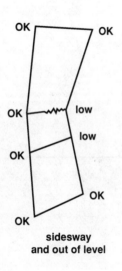

sidesway
and out of level

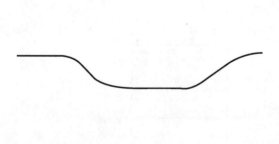

10.

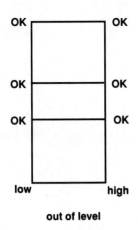

out of level

Job Sheet 11-1

Name_____ Date _____ Instructor Review _____

Universal Bench Mounting

Objective

After completing this lab, the student should be able to safely mount a unibody car on a bench.

Equipment

Unibody car
Impact wrench
Bench with clamps

Safety Equipment

Safety glasses

Procedure

**Task
Completed**

1. Read the instruction guide on mounting the vehicle. Some benches are assembled under the car. In other cases, the car is raised up and the bench is rolled under the car. These instructions will be for the latter case.   ❏

2. Safely raise the vehicle to bench clearance height. A properly designed lift is the best. Some manufacturers use a flow jack and wheel stands.   ❏

3. Roll the bench under the car. Orientate the pinch weld clamps so that they will be in the proper location. Lock the clamps in place.   ❏

4. Lower the car down to the pinch weld clamps. Make sure that the clamp does not crush a brake line or a gas line.   ❏

5. Use an impact wrench to tighten the clamp bolts. When the car is securely mounted on the bench, the bench and the car may be moved.   ❏

6. Consult the manual provided by the bench manufacturer to determine locations to mount fixtures, pins or targets.   ❏

7. Any fixture or pin that does not reach the intended point indicates damage.   ❏

8. Record any deviations and make a damage diagram.   ❏

Job Sheet 11-2

Name_____ Date _____ Instructor Review _____

Unibody Tie Downs

Objective

After completing this lab, the student should be able to properly lift and clamp a unibody vehicle.

Equipment

Unibody vehicle
Pinch clamps
Bar
Floor jack
Jack stands

Safety Equipment

Safety glasses

Procedure

The purpose of tie downs is to immobilize the vehicle. A proper tie down will aid in correcting the damage. An improper tie down may increase damage to the vehicle. Unibody vehicles are normally tied down by bolting clamps to the bottom of the rocker panels. The clamps are chained to the floor or bolted to the bed of a frame machine.

Task Completed

1. Read the installation directions for the type of system you have. Follow these directions. If there aren't any directions, use the following: ❑

2. Check the rocker panel pinch flange for brake, gas lines or wires. It may be necessary to unbolt and move any obstructions. Place A clamp at each torque box. Place the front clamps as far forward as possible. On some vehicle it may be necessary to unbolt the bottom of the fenders to move them out for clearance. ❑

3. Install the rear clamps as far back as possible. Use an air impact wrench to tighten the bolts. ❑

4. Slide the bar into the two front clamps. Put the remaining bar between the two rear clamps. ❑

5. Jack up the front of the vehicle with a floor jack under the front bar. Raise to the proper height. Put Jack stands under both sides of the bar. ❑

6. Raise the rear of the vehicle in the same manner. Place a jack stand at either end of the bar. ❑

7. Wrap a chain around the bar at each jack stand. For a front pull, anchor the chain to the floor toward the rear of the vehicle. For rear pulls, anchor toward the front of the vehicle. On side pulls, anchor on the side opposite of the pull. ❑

Job Sheet 11-3

Name_____ Date _____ Instructor Review _____

Truck Tie Down

Objective

After completing this lab, the student should be able to properly tie down a pickup truck for a frame pull.

Equipment

Pickup truck
Frame chains
Jack stands
Floor jack

Safety Equipment

Safety glasses

Procedure

	Task Completed
1. Proper truck tie downs will aid in frame repair. Poor tie downs will damage the vehicle or hurt the workers. Always plan out the proper tie downs.	❏
2. Four jack stands are placed under the truck frame. The vehicle needs to be high enough that the suspension is unloaded. Usually two stands are near a cross member under the cowl and two are near a cross member at the front of the bed. However, this may not work for all trucks. Your instructor will tell you where to place the stands.	❏
3. Your instructor will demonstrate how to safely raise the truck with the floor jack.	❏
4. Place the jack stands in the desired locations. Lower the truck onto the stands.	❏
5. Usually the tie down is made at each floor jack by wrapping the frame with a chain. This prevents the frame from moving in any direction.	❏
6. Put the ends together on six-foot length of frame chain. This forms a loop. From under the vehicle, slip the loop over the frame so the loop hangs down on the outside of the rail. Put one end of the chain through the loop and anchor it to the floor or bed of the frame machine. The other end of the chain also goes through the loop and is anchored at a right angle to the first chain.	❏
7. An anchor should be placed at each jack stand. The vehicle is now secured for pulling.	❏
8. If an area of the frame is high, the jack stand can be left out of this spot. Just tie it down. As the pull is made, it will tend to lower this area.	❏
9. As you pull, always check the anchors for distortion of the frame rails.	❏

Job Sheet 11-4

Name_____ Date _____ Instructor Review _____

Front Damaged Unibody Repair

Objective

The student should be able to measure, tie down, hook up, pull and stress relieve a front hit unibody.

Equipment

Obtain a front hit unibody in need of a
   pull in the rad support and apron.
Frame machine
Tie down system
Hammers
Tram
Frame dimension guide
Hand tools

Safety Equipment

Safety glasses
Welding tinted face shield
Long sleeves
High-top shoes

Task Completed

Prcoedure

1. Remove the radiator, fan motor, and A/C condensor. If the A/C is charged, drain the refrigerant in an approved manner. When you break open the A/C lines, be sure to cap off the system to prevent moisture damage.   ❑

2. Remove the front bumpers, grille, headlights and header panel. Leave the hood and fenders on for now.   ❑

3. Mount the car on the frame machine. Hang the gauges and take measurements. Draw a damage diagram in the space below. Write in what the measurements should be and what they actually are.   ❑

4. Draw a diagram showing the tie downs, hook ups and pull sequence.   ❑

5. Tie the vehicle down.   ❑

6. Examine the buckles. Kinked, high strength, steel parts must be replaced. Bent, high strength, steel parts may be straightened. Make a drawing of the structural parts and indicate where the kink and bends are located. Explain which parts will be replaced and which parts will be repaired.   ❑

_____

_____

_____

_____

_____

7. Read pages 387–388 in your textbook about heating high strength steel. Treat all structural parts as high strength steel. Follow the text guidelines for temperature and time of heating.   ❑

8. Place the clamps. Make a pull. Put tension on the damaged part. A spring hammer buckles; do not bend the buckles over. Apply more tension. Use the sequence of pull, tension, stop, hammer, and pull. Correct mash first, then the sidesway, followed by the height.   ❑

**Task
Completed**

9. If the pull is not going as planned, stop and rethink the procedure. ❑

10. Make a measurement to check the progress. You can also close the hood to see how it lines up. ❑

11. When the measurements are correct, remove the fenders and hood to prepare for radiator support removal. ❑

Job Sheet 11-5

Name_____ Date _____ Instructor Review _____

Damaged Cowl Repair

Objective

After completing this lab, the student should be able to measure and align a damaged cowl.

Equipment

Cowl damaged vehicle
Frame machine
Tram gauge
Frame dimension book
Hinge pillar pull tool

Safety Equipment

Safety glasses
Dust respirator
Leather gloves

Procedure

Task Completed

1. Carefully examine the damaged vehicle. Dowl damage is present if the front door drops as it is opened or if the window frame is tilted out at the top. Check the roof for pressure dents.   ❑

2. Mount the car on the frame machine and tie it down. Hang the gauges. Make a damage diagram. Remove the damaged door. Use a tram gauge to X check the door. Consult a frame dimension book for specific measurements. Make a damage diagram of the door. If the car was hit from the side, remove the dash to check for hidden damage.   ❑

3. Plan out the hook ups and pulls on the diagrams. If the cowl was pushed far enough, you will need to attach a hinge pillar pull tool to the cowl and pull directly on it, as you pull on the upper frame rail. Less severe cowl damage can be pulled by attaching to the upper frame rail only.   ❏

4. If the cowl was hit from the side, an L-shaped hook can be used to pull the cowl out. Hits of this nature can be quite difficult to repair.   ❏

5. Attach the clamps, tools or hooks. Position the towers and chains. Apply tension and stop.   ❏

6. Spring hammer the buckles. Start with the buckles, popped paint and spot welds that are farthest away from the damage. A block of wood can be used to spread the force of the hammer. Do not pound the buckles flat.   ❏

7. If the metal does not move according to the plan, stop and rethink the procedure.   ❏

8. Measure the door opening. Continue pulling until the dimensions are correct. Hang a replacement door to check the fit.   ❏

9. If the fit is correct and the hinge pillar is not kinked and does not need any refinishing, the door may be left in place. Otherwise, remove the door.   ❏

10. If the hinge pillar is kinked and needs replacement, drill out the spot welds and use the recommended procedure to splice.   ❏

Job Sheet 11-6

Name_____ Date _____ Instructor Review _____

Damaged Roof Rail Repair

Objective

After completing this lab, the student should be able to measure and push roof rails back into shape.

Equipment

Rolled over vehicle
4 ton porto power set
Frame machine
Frame gauges
Dimension manual
Tram gauge

Safety Equipment

Safety glasses

Procedure

Task Completed

1. Mount the vehicle on a frame machine. Hang the gauges and check for frame damage. Make a damage diagram.   ❏

2. Remove the seats, carpet, doors, windshield and back glass. Clean up any broken glass.   ❏

3. Tram measure the windshield, back glass and door openings. Record the data. Check for kinks, popped paint and buckles._____   ❏

    _____

    _____

    _____

4. Consult a frame dimension manual for the proper size of the windshield, backdoor glass and door openings. Decide on a repair plan. Any frame damage must be corrected first. If the frame was damaged and repaired, recheck the upper body measurements.   ❏

5. A porto power will be used to move the roof. Set it up inside the car. Prevent additional damage to the vehicle by spreading out the force of the porto power. Use a block of wood at the roof rail or header. Base the porto power set in a solid area with a block of wood.   ❏

6. Do not push one part back to the proper location all at once. Gradually push one rail, then switch to another rail. Always work all of the rails out together.   ❏

7. Use spring hammering under tension to normalize the metal.   ❏

8. To get a bowed center pillar up, you may need to pull in at the bowed area with a tower. Set the porto power set to push up where the roof meets the pillar. Work the tower and the porto power in unison.   ❏

9. When the dimensions are correct, hang the doors and check for fit. Also test fit the windshield and back glass.   ❏

10. If all of the parts fit, you can cut the roof skin and replace it. Any kinked structural parts must be replaced.   ❏

Job Sheet 11-7

Name_____ Date _____ Instructor Review _____

Side Damaged Repair

Objective

After completing this lab, the student should be able to measure and repair a center pillar and rocker panel.

Equipment

Center hit vehicle
Frame machine
Dimension guide
Frame gauges

Safety Equipment

Safety glasses

Procedure

Task Completed

1. Remove the doors, seats, carpet and headliner. Clean up any broken glass. ❏

2. Mount the vehicle on a frame machine. Hang gauges. Make a damage diagram. Measure the distance between the center pillars. Consult a frame dimension manual for proper measurement. Measure the length of the damaged rocker panel. Compare this to the standard. Check for kinks, buckles and popped paint in the floor, roof and center pillar. ❏

3. Check for door gaps on the undamaged side. If they are wider than normal, the car may have a "banana hit." In this severe damage situation, one side is shorter than normal and the other side is longer than normal. A lighter hit does not cause a "banana hit." ❏

4. Decide on a repair plan. If the car is "banana hit," plan a hook up at the front of the vehicle. The anchor should be placed in front at the opposite side of the car. The chain connecting the anchor and the hook up should form a 45 degree angle with the front of the car. In this way, as the damaged side is pulled, the anchor tends to lengthen the damaged side and shorten the undamaged side. A similar hook up/anchor should be made at the rear of the vehicle. If the damage is not a severe "banana hit," the rocker panel can be lengthened by pushing the pinch weld clamps apart with a ten ton porto power. Another method is a double stretch pull with one tower at each end, pulling away from each other.   ❏

5. Sometimes it is difficult to grab the rocker panel to pull it out. The outer rocker may be cut out and bolted on a pull clamp. There are tools that wrap around the rocker and clamp at the floor. Use at least two hookups to pull the rocker and the floor.   ❏

6. To pull the center pillar, a nylon strap may be wrapped around it. Use a block of wood that is wider than the pillar to keep the strap from crushing the pillar as the strap is tightened.   ❏

7. Make the planned hookups and line up the towers. Apply tension. Spring hammer any buckles on the floor. Do not pound on the buckles. Work from the undamaged area outward to the damaged area. Lengthen the rocker as you pull out.   ❏

8. A porto power may need to be placed inside the car to raise the center pillar. Position the porto power base at the opposite side of the center pillar. Brace the porto power with a block of wood. Push up and out as the tension is applied to the floor and center pillar. Spring hammer the center pillar.   ❏

9. Check measurements as you work. When the measurements are correct, remove the panels that will be replaced. Metal finish the roof damage.   ❏

Job Sheet 11-8

Name_____ Date _____ Instructor Review _____

Unibody Rear Rail

Objective

After completing this lab, the student should be able to measure, pull and align a rear hit unibody.

Equipment

Rear hit unibody car
Frame machine
Tie down equipment
Gauges
Tram gauge
Pull clamp
Cut off tool

Safety Equipment

Safety glasses

Procedure

Task Completed

1. Closely examine the damaged vehicle. Check for gaps, including the hood and front doors for misalignment. If the damage is severe, remove the back seat and check for buckles or popped paint in the floor.   ❏

2. Mount the vehicle on the frame machine using the pinch weld clamps. Hang the gauges and diagnose the damage. Fill out a damage diagram. Remove the tail lights and rear bumper.   ❏

3. Plan out the hook-ups and pulls. Decide where the clamps will be placed, where the towers will be located and how the metal is expected to move. Draw the plan on the damage diagram.   ❏

4. Install the clamps. You may need to cut a hole into the rear body panel to grab the trunk floor. Use an impact wrench to tighten the clamps. Move the towers into place and attach the chains.   ❏

5. Begin the pulls by applying tension according to the plan. Spring hammer the buckles or creases farthest away from the impact. Do not pound the buckles flat. Spring hammer, then apply more tension. As you apply tension, you will give the metal a direction to move. As you spring hammer, you will coax the metal into following the tension.   ❏

6. If the metal does not move according to the plan, stop and rethink the procedure.   ❏

7. As you apply tension, check the rear door gaps for alignment. Relieve all tension in the unibody by spring hammering. Work out the buckles in the quarter panel with hammer and dolly. Check the deck lid for fit.   ❏

8. Check the gauges. When the length is correct, remove the sidesway. Then set the proper height.   ❏

9. Any kinked structural parts must be replaced.   ❏

Job Sheet 11-9

Name_____ Date _____ Instructor Review _____

Shock Tower Alignment

Objective

After completing this lab, the student should be able to measure and pull a damaged shock tower to specification.

Equipment

Front end vehicle with shock tower
    movement
Frame machine
Frame gauges

Safety Equipment

Safety glasses

Procedure

Task Completed

1. Remove the hood, fenders, front bumpers, radiator and condensor.   ❑

2. Mount the vehicle on a frame machine. Hang the gauges, including the strut tower measuring gauge. Make a diagram of the damage.   ❑

3. Check the aprons, rails and strut towers for kinks, buckles and popped paint. Then check the deck lid and door gaps. Also check the roof for pressure dents.   ❑

4. Decide on a repair plan. Determine where the hookups and the towers will be placed. Work from the undamaged area out to the point of impact,   ❑

5. Many times the strut towers are rolled in or tipped back. To bring them back to the proper place, the McPherson strut is removed. A strut tower tool is then bolted into the holes. A hook up is made to the tool so that it can be pulled out or forward.   ❑

Task Completed

6. Make the planned hook ups on the rails and pull to apply tension. Spring hammer to normalize the metal. Do not pound directly on the buckles. Use tension and light hammering.   ❏

7. If there are not any kinks or bends in the cowl or behind the shock tower, you can hook up to the tower and pull it into position. This is done after tension is applied to move the rails.   ❏

8. Measure the position of the towers with the shock tower gauge.   ❏

Job Sheet 11-10

Name_____ Date _____ Instructor Review _____

Pickup Diamond and Twist Repair

Objective

After completing this lab, the student should be able to diagnose and repair diamond and twist damage.

Equipment

Truck with diamond damage
Truck with twist damage
Frame machine and gauges

Safety Equipment

Safety glasses

Procedure

Task Completed

1. Examine the truck for damage. A quick way to check for damage is to sight the tail gate into the cab Rear glass. Out of level may indicate twist. Compare the gap between the cab and the bed on one side with the other side. A difference may mean diamond. ❏

2. Use a tram gauge under the cab. Make an X check of holes in the same position on one rail as the other rail. Do not use the cab mount bolts. A difference in measurements greater than ¼" indicates diamond. Make a damage diagram. ❏

3. Hang a frame gauge under the cowl and another at the rear of the cab. Move at least ten feet away from the truck and sight the gauges. Any difference in level indicates twist. Add this information to the damage diagram. ❏

4. We will repair each of these problems separately. In an actual repair, if both are present, they can be corrected together. ❏

5. An impact that drives one rail back relative to the other rail causes diamond. To repair diamond, mount the truck on jack stands. Make the tie downs on the undamaged rail near the cowl and the front of the bed. Do not tie down the damaged rail. Pull the damaged rail forward. ❏

6. Make a hook up on the damaged rail near the cowl and pull forward. If this cannot be made, hook up at the front of the damaged rail and pull forward, Overpull slightly to compensate for a settle back.   ❑

7. A true twist extending through the entire vehicle means one corner is low and the same corner on the opposite side is high. To correct this problem, place jack stands under the cowl and tie it down so it can not move. Place a jack stand under the low rear corner of the cab. Do not tie it down.   ❑

8. Pull down the high ends and the high under-cab area. Push up on the low ends.   ❑

Review Questions

Name_____ Date _____ Instructor Review _____

1. Technician A states that on a unibody, a single pull is best. Technician B believes that on a unibody, multiple pulls are best. Who is correct?

   A. Technician A
   B. Technician B
   C. Both A and B
   D. Neither A nor B

2. The anchoring force must be stronger than the pull force.

   A. True
   B. False

3. Technician A states that a unibody must have at least two undamaged reference points to set up measurements. Technician B believes that when you straighten a full frame, usually the suspension will be in alignment. Who is correct?

   A. Technician A
   B. Technician B
   C. Both A and B
   D. Neither A nor B

4. Technician A states that portable frame pullers can be set up quickly. Technician B believes that portable frame pullers are safer than rack systems. Who is correct?

   A. Technician A
   B. Technician B
   C. Both A and B
   D. Neither A nor B

5. It is dangerous to stand in line with a chain under tension.
   A. True
   B. False

6. Technician A overpulls slightly to compensate for settle back. Technician B believes that excessive overpulling will cause problems. Who is correct?

   A. Technician A
   B. Technician B
   C. Both A and B
   D. Neither A nor B

7. The proper sequence of repair is length, then _____ followed by

   _____.

8. The proper repair method to straighten a unibody is to pull, hold and pull.

   A. True
   B. False

9. Technician A heats unibody rails on the corners. Technician B heats in the center of the unibody rail. Who is correct?

   A. Technician A
   B. Technician B
   C. Both A and B
   D. Neither A nor B

10. Technician A states that if a HSLA structural panel is kinked, it must be replaced. Technician B believes that if a structural panel is bent, it can be straightened. Who is correct?

    A. Technician A
    B. Technician B
    C. Both A and B
    D. Neither A nor B

Shop Assignment 12-1

Name_____ Date _____ Instructor Review _____

Panel Misalignments

Examine the following vehicles and indicate what the problem is and how to correct it.

Equipment

A car with parking lot dings or hail damage

Safety Equipment

Safety glasses

1.

_____
_____
_____
_____
_____
_____
_____

2.

_____
_____
_____
_____
_____
_____
_____

3.

_____
_____
_____
_____
_____
_____
_____

4.

_____
_____
_____
_____
_____
_____
_____

5.

_____
_____
_____
_____
_____
_____
_____

6.

_____
_____
_____
_____
_____
_____
_____
_____

7.

_____
_____
_____
_____
_____
_____
_____

8.

_____
_____
_____
_____
_____
_____
_____
_____

9.

_____
_____
_____
_____
_____
_____
_____

10.

_____

_____

_____

_____

_____

_____

_____

_____

Job Sheet 12-1

Name_____ Date _____ Instructor Review _____

Weld an A Pillar

Objective

After completing this lab, the student should be able to weld an A pillar.

Equipment

Scrap A pillar or windshield post
Grinder
MIG welder
Weld-through primer
Hack saw
Drill
$5/16$" bit

Safety Equipment

Safety glasses
Welding helmet with #10 shade
Welding gloves
Welding sleeves
Welding respirator
High-top shoes

Procedure

Task Completed

1. Consult your textbook, pages 411 and 415, for the procedure. Cut an A pillar in half. Avoid reinforced areas. Cut one inch off of the end. This will be the insert. Drill out spot welds and separate the pieces. Cut the pieces to fit inside the pillar. ❏

2. Drill the plug weld holes into pillar pieces. Remove the paint from the insert pieces. Spray with weld through primer. Slide the insert pieces into one pillar piece. ❏

3. Slip the remaining pillar piece over the insert. Leave a $1/8$" gap between the pillar pieces. ❏

4. Weld the plug holes first. ❏

5. Use skip welding to form a continuous bead around the entire joint. ❏

Job Sheet 12-2

Name_____ Date _____ Instructor Review _____

Weld a Rocker Panel

Objective

After completing this lab, the student should be able to properly splice and weld a rocker panel.

Equipment

18" section of salvage rocker panel
Reciprocating saw
Spot welder cutter
Weld-through primer
MIG welder
$^5/_{16}$" drill bit
Abrasive wheel

Safety Equipment

Safety glasses
Welding helmet with #10 shade
Welding gloves
Welding sleeves
Welding respirator
High-top shoes

Procedure

Task Completed

1. Measure in six inches from each end of the rocker panel. Mark at the six inch lines. Cut at the marks with a reciprocating saw. This will give you a center piece and two ends. ❏

2. Measure the cross section of the rocker panel. The inserts cut from the two ends should be twice the width of the cross section. If the rocker is two inches wide in the cross section, each insert should be four inches long. Measure and cut off the inserts. ❏

3. The inserts should have the corners cut out (see page 00 in your textbook). Remove the paint with an abrasive wheel. Do not remove the galvanizing. Spray with a weld-through primer. ❏

4. Drill out the spot welds from the center piece. Be careful to cut only the outer piece. Do not cut a hole through both pieces. If you do, you will not have anything on which to weld. You should now have the center piece separated into inner and outer pieces. ❏

5. Mark the location for $^5/_{16}$" plug weld holes in the two end pieces. The holes should be $^3/_4$" away from the edge and $^3/_4$" apart. Drill the holes. Remove the burrs from the back side. ❏

6. Test fit the inserts in the two end pieces. When they fit correctly, clamp them tightly. Set up, tune and test the MIG welder. Weld the plug holes. ❏

7. Drill plug weld holes into the two center pieces. They should be made the same way as the holes on the end pieces. Remove the burrs from the back side. ❏

8. Align the end pieces and the center pieces. The gap between an end piece
    and the center piece should be the same as the thickness of the panel. Clamp
    together.   ❏

9. Weld all the plug holes. Then skip weld the butt joints.   ❏

10. Dress the welds.   ❏

Job Sheet 12-3

Name_____ Date _____ Instructor Review _____

Vehicle Dissection

Objective

After completing this lab, the student should be able to remove and install metal parts.

Equipment

Unibody car
Tape measure
Tram
Hand tools

Safety Equipment

Safety glasses

Procedure

Task Completed

1. Obtain a unibody car. Inspect the vehicle. Examine all gaps between panels. Note any problems. Open the hood and X check to see if it is square. ❑

2. Remove the front bumper, grille, header panel, hood and fenders. ❑

3. Remove the doors by unbolting the doors from the hinges. Leave the hinges on the cowl. If the hinges are welded on, remove the spring. Then pound out the pin. If the doors are powered, you'll need to remove the door trim panels and unhook any electrical connections. Feed the wires out of the doors. ❑

4. Remove the rear bumpers, tail lights, and deck lid. ❑

5. Begin the reassembly by installing the doors. On a power door, feed the wires into the door. It's easier to install doors with two people, one holding the door with the other person bolting it on. If only one person is available, use a floor jack to support the rear edge of the door. Bolt the door on or install the pins. Close the door. Check for alignment at the bottom of the door. A uniform gap between the door and the rocker panel means that the door is hanging straight. Check for a uniform gap at the windshield pillar and door. If these two gaps are not uniform, adjust the hinges until they are. Check to see if the doors open and close properly. Reinstall the electrical hookups. Check for power operation. ❑

6. Install the hood. The installation is easier with two people, one person on each side. If only one person is available, tape cardboard to the rear corners of the hood. This will prevent damage to the windshield if the hood slips. Set the hood in place and raise. Use the prop rod to hold it open. The hood should be wedged in place. Bolt the hinges on. Check for a uniform gap between the hood and the cowl vent panel or windshield. If this gap is uniform in width, the hood is on correctly. Check to see if the hood opens and closes properly. ❑

7. Install the fenders next. Check for a uniform gap between the fender and the hood and the fender and the door. Move the fender until even gaps are obtained. Tighten the fender bolts. ❑

8. Install the header or grille and the front bumper. Check the bumper for level. Adjust if needed. ❑

9. Install the deck lid, tail lights and rear bumper. Check the deck lid for uniform
    gaps and proper height. The deck lid should be level to the quarter panels.   ❑

10. Fill out this chart: ❑

Panel   **Where to Check for a Fit**

Door   _____

Hood   _____

Fender   _____

Front bumper   . _____

Deck lid   _____

Rear bumper   _____

Job Sheet 12-4

Name_____ Date _____ Instructor Review _____

Power Door Disassembly

Objective

After completing this lab, the student should be able to disassemble and reassemble a power door.

Equipment

Vehicle with power door
Hand tools

Safety Equipment

Safety glasses

Procedure

Task Completed

1. Obtain a car with power windows and power door locks.   ❑

2. Remove the trim panel. Usually it is held in place with clips around the edge. Sometimes the arm rest must be unbolted. There may also be a screw in the trim panel behind the door handle. Unplug any electrical connections.   ❑

3. Remove the plastic dust shield. Raise or lower the window until the bolts or rivets that hold the glass to the regulator are visible inside the door.   ❑

4. Unbolt or drill out the rivets. Unbolt the window channel. Pull the window out of the channel and remove the window. Also remove the channel. See your instructor if you are having difficulties.   ❑

5. Locate the power window regulator and the power door actuator. Unplug them.   ❑

6. Unbolt or drill out the rivets holding the regulator and the actuator. Disconnect the actuator from the door lock. Remove through the loading holes.   ❑

7. Remove the door handle and the door latch. These are connected by rods. Be sure to notice how they are oriented.   ❑

8. Begin reassembly by installing the door handle and latch. Put the rods in place. Check for proper operation.   ❑

9. Install the regulator and the actuator. Use ¼" rivets if the parts were riveted in. Hook up the actuator to the door lock. Plug in the electrical connections.   ❑

10. Slide the window and window channel into place. Bolt or rivet into place. Check for proper operation.   ❑

11. Glue or tape the plastic dust shield to the door. Snap on the door trim panel.   ❑

Job Sheet 12-5

Name_____ Date _____ Instructor Review _____

Flanged Panel Splice

Objective

After completing this lab, the student should be able to weld two panels together with a flange joint.

Equipment

Fender
MIG welder
Sheet metal screws
Sand blaster
Grinder
Cut off tool
Weld-through primer
Sealer
Metal file

Safety Equipment

Safety glasses
Dust respirator
Leather gloves
Welding helmet with #10 shade
Welding gloves
Welding sleeves
Welding respirator
High-top shoes

Procedure

Task Completed

1. Locate an area on the fender that is uniform in width. ❏

2. Grind the paint off of a two inch strip. Use a cut-off tool to cut the panel in half, down the middle of the bare metal. ❏

3. Flange the edge of one of the halves. If there is a sharp wheel well, cut on the corner and flange around it. ❏

4. Grind the back side of the overlap piece. Apply weld through primer to all of the bare metal. ❏

5. Lay the overlap panel on the flanged panel. Leave a $1/8$" gap between the overlap panel and the corner of the flange. ❏

6. Drill $1/8$" holes through both panels at every inch. Install sheet metal screws to hold the panels together. ❏

7. Sand blast the weld area. Tune and test the welder. MIG weld, using the skip method. ❏

8. Remove the screws and weld the holes shut. ❏

9. Grind the welds to contour. Metal file to find the high and low spots. Pick and file any problem areas. ❏

10. Apply sealer to the back side of the joint. ❏

Job Sheet 12-6

Name_____ Date _____ Instructor Review _____

Butt Weld Splice Panel

Objective

After completing this lab, the student should be able to butt weld two panels together.

Equipment

Fender
Grinder
Cut off tool
MIG welder
Welding clamps
Metal file
Hammer and dolly

Safety Equipment

Safety glasses
Dust respirator
Leather gloves
Welding helmet with #10 shade
Welding gloves
Welding sleeves
Welding respirator
High-top shoes

Procedure

Task Completed

1. Obtain a medium crown fender. Grind off the paint in a 2" x 2" area. ❑

2. Use a cut-off tool to cut out a 1" x 1" square of metal inside the bare metal area. ❑

3. Cut out a piece of bare metal to fit the square hole. Hammer and dolly into the proper contour. There should be no larger than a $1/16$" gap between the patch piece and hole edge. ❑

4. Clamp the patch piece in place. If weld clamps will not fit, you can use masking tape to hold the piece away from the weld area. ❑

5. Tune and test the welder. Tack weld by striking an arc on the patch piece and continuing the weld onto the edge of the hole. Tack weld in the center of each patch piece side. Next, tack weld in each corner. ❑

6. Skip weld the gaps by working on one side and then on the opposite side. Beware of heat buildup and panel warpage. ❑

7. Grind the weld down. ❑

8. Metal file to find the high and low spots. ❑

9. Hammer and dolly, or pick and file to the proper contour. ❑

Job Sheet 12-7

Name_____ Date _____ Instructor Review _____

Quarter Panel Replacement

Objective

After completing this lab, the student should be able to splice a quarter panel.

Equipment

MIG welder/grinder
Flange tool
Cut off tool
Spot weld cutter
Repair manual
Splatter paint
Epoxy primer
Heavy bodied sealer

Safety Equipment

Safety glasses
Dust respirator
Leather gloves
Welding helmet with #10 shade
Welding gloves
Welding sleeves
Welding respirator
High-top shoes

Procedure

Task Completed

1. Obtain a body repair manual for the vehicle you are working on. The manual will list the recommended splice locations and the type of joints. If a manual is unavailable, follow this sequence for splicing a quarter panel. Decide on the cut location and scribe a rough cut line.   ❏

2. Remove the rear bumper, tail light, and trim. Locate the spot welds on the wheel arch, inside the gas door (if there is one), inside the door, inside the trunk, on the rear body panel, and on the flange behind the rear wheel. Center punch the spot welds. Drill a 1/8" pilot hole in the welds. Cut out the welds with a spot weld cutter. Rough cut the damaged quarter panel with a cut off tool. Stay at least two inches away from the rough cut line. Hammer and dolly any damaged areas to the proper contour.   ❏

3. Examine the replacement quarter panel for dents. Scribe a final cut line on this quarter panel. Cut at the line with a cut off tool.   ❏

4. This is the critical step. Once the damaged quarter panel is cut to fit the replacement quarter, any mistakes made in measuring will be difficult to correct. Put the replacement quarter panel on the car. Check for fit with the deck lid, tail light and door. When you are satisfied with the fit, Scribe a line on the damaged quarter panel using the final cut line edge on the replacement quarter panel as a guide.   ❏

5. Measure $1/2$" in from this scribed line. This gives a $1/2$" overlap for the flange. This is the final cut line. Cut on this line with a cut off tool. Grind off the paint. It is easier to grind now than after the panel is flanged.   ❏

6. Flange the panel using a suitable tool. Use the edge as a guide. Apply weld through primer to the flanged joint. Grind the weld areas on the replacement panel. Apply weld through primer to these areas. Punch plug weld holes using the same number and location as the factory spot welds. In areas that the flange tool can not reach, support the rear edge with a dinging spoon and lightly tap down the flanged area.   ❏

7. Fit up the replacement panel. Check all gaps. When the fit is perfect, drill $1/8$" holes every two inches through both panels in the flange area. Install sheet metal screws. Clamps can be used to hold the metal together in other areas. If clamps can not reach, use screws.   ❏

8. Tune and test the welder. Weld the replacement panel. Start with the plug welds. Do not overheat the panel. On the flange joint, start in the center. Then skip weld.   ❏

9. Dress the welds with a grinder. Grind only in the weld, not the surrounding metal.   ❏

10. On the inside of the flange joint, remove all of the weld scale and blistered paint. Scuff the inside of the replacement panel. Spray with epoxy primer. After it has dried, use a heavy-bodied sealer to protect the joint. Apply splatter paint.   ❏

Job Sheet 12-8

Name_____ Date _____ Instructor Review _____

Door Skin Replacement

Objective

After completing this lab, the student should be able to replace a door skin.

Equipment

Door in need of skin replacement
Door skin bonding adhesive
Hammer and dolly
MIG welder
Flange tool
Metal file
DA
Grinder

Safety Equipment

Safety glasses
Dust respirator
Leather gloves
Welding helmet with #10 shade
Welding gloves
Welding sleeves
Welding respirator
High-top shoes

Procedure

Task Completed

1. Remove the door from the car. Also remove the handles, trim pad, and glass. Disconnect any electrical wires. ❑

2. Use a grinder on the hem flange. Grind down the area where the outer panel is bent double. ❑

3. Cut off the skin on the window frame as close to the door as possible. ❑

4. Cut off any tabs on the inside of the window opening. ❑

5. Remove the skin. Be careful of any sharp edges. ❑

6. Determine the window frame splice location and flange the window frame panel. Prep the tabs for weld. ❑

7. Test the fit of the new skin. Line up the body lines. ❑

8. Apply the primer and urethane bond as per kit instructions. ❑

9. Install the skin with proper alignment. ❑

10. Fold over the hem flange. The most important step is to always support the door edge with a dolly. Always hit on the dolly. Fold the hem half-way all the way around. Then come back and fold the remaining distance as on page 426 in your textbook. ❑

11. Weld the flange joint and tabs as needed. ❑

12. Use a metal file to locate high spots on the outside edge of the door. ❑

13. Use 80 grit paper on a dual-action sander, set at grind mode. Smooth over the outside edge of the door. Check for high and low areas. ❑

Job Sheet 12-9

Name_____ Date _____ Instructor Review _____

Radiator Support Replacement

Objective

After completing this lab, the student should be able to properly remove and replace a radiator support.

Equipment

Front end damaged unibody,
   pulled back to specification
Spot weld cutter bits
Drill
$5/_{16}$" drill bit
Grinder
Tram
Weld-through primer
Nylon wheel
Hand tools

Safety Equipment

Safety glasses
Dust respirator
Leather gloves
Welding helmet with #10 shade
Welding gloves
Welding sleeves
Welding respirator
High-top shoes

Procedure

Task Completed

1. Remove the fenders, front bumpers, grille, headlights, A/C condensor, radiator, and fan motor. ❑

2. Make an X check of the hood opening. Hang the gauges and check for sag. Any frame damage or buckles in the apron must be corrected before the radiator support is removed. ❑

3. Locate and center punch spot welds. Drill pilot holes in the welds with a ⅛" drill bit. Cut the welds out with a spot weld cutter bit. Cut through the outer panel only. This will be difficult to do. Proceed slowly. As soon as the upper panel loosens, stop drilling. If you cannot reach the welds to drill them, you may be able to cut the metal around the weld with an air chisel. Dress down the remaining weld with a grinder or cut-off tool. ❑

4. When all of the welds are removed, the radiator support can be pulled out. Use a grinder to remove the spot weld nuggets on the radiator. Support flanges where the radiator support was welded. Spray bare metal areas with weld-through primer. ❑

5. Prep replacement support by drilling or punching ⁵⁄₁₆" holes in the same location as the original support welds. Use the same number of welds as in the original. Use a nylon wheel to remove primer from the area around each hole. Spray weld through primer on all bare metal areas. ❑

6. Clamp the replacement support in place. Make an X check. Hang the fenders and the hood. Check for proper gaps. Install the hood latch and check for proper hood operation. Check level with frame gauges and make any needed adjustments. Remove the fenders and latch. Prop the hood open.   ❏

7. Use a spot sand blaster to remove weld-through primer in the plug weld holes. Cover the windshield and engine with a welding blanket. Tune the welder and test a practice plug weld. Avoid excessive heat build-up when you weld. This is accomplished by welding one or two holes in one area and then switching to a different area.   ❏

8. Dress welds with a cut-off wheel. Be sure to grind on the weld only, not on the surrounding metal.   ❏

Job Sheet 12-10

Name_____ Date _____ Instructor Review _____

Splice Frame Rail

Objective

After completing this lab, the student should be able to properly splice a frame rail.

Equipment

Section of frame rail
Saw
Sand blaster
Weld-through primer
MIG welder

Safety Equipment

Safety glasses
Dust respirator
Leather gloves
Welding helmet with #10 shade
Welding gloves
Welding sleeves
Welding respirator
High-top shoes

Tech Cor researches proper autobody repair methods. They have written several excellent guides for frame rail splicing on particular vehicles. If you have a vehicle in need of a frame rail splice, contact Tech Cor at 1-800-780-8055, 100 E. Palatine Road, Wheeling IL 60090 to see if they have a repair procedure available.

The following exercise is designed to give the student practice in rail replacement. It is not intended to cover any specific model of car.

Procedure

Task Completed

1. Obtain a section of lower frame rail from a unibody car. ❑

2. Measure to the center of the rail and mark a line around the entire rail. ❑

3. Cut the rail at the line with a reciprocating saw or a cut-off wheel. ❑

4. At the cut line and inward 1", remove the paint from the outside of one piece. Do the same to the inside of the other piece. ❑

5. Use a cut-off wheel or hack saw to cut out the corners on each piece. Spray weld-through primer on bare metal. ❑

6. Slide the piece with the paint removed from the inside over the piece with the paint removed from the outside. The overlap should be at least 1/4". ❑

7. Sand blast off the primer in the weld area. Tune the welder and test a practice weld. Clamp the piece assembly to a welding fixture. This will allow you to make flat, vertical and overhead welds. ❑

8. Weld the pieces together using the skip method. ❑

Review Questions

Name_____ Date _____ Instructor Review _____

1. Technician A states that a properly sectioned frame rail has all the crush characteristics of a new rail. Technician B believes that full replacement of a rail is the only acceptable repair method. Who is correct?

   A. Technician A
   B. Technician B
   C. Both A and B
   D. Neither A nor B

2. Technician A cuts spot welds with a hole saw. Technician B uses a drill bit. Who is correct?

   A. Drill bit. Who is correct?
   B. Technician B
   C. Both A and B
   D. Neither A nor B

3. Technician A uses a cutting torch to remove panels. Technician B uses an air chisel to remove panels. Who is correct?

   A. Technician A
   B. Technician B
   C. Both A and B
   D. Neither A nor B

4. No frame rails should be cut off until the frame is straight.

   A. True
   B. False

5. Technician A uses a grinder to remove paint from an area to be welded. Technician B uses a disk sander in the same situation. Who is correct?

   A. Technician A
   B. Technician B
   C. Both A and B
   D. Neither A nor B

6. An insert should be _____ the width of the cross section.

7. Technician A bonds the replacement door skin to the door frame. Technician B welds the replacement door skin to the door frame. Who is correct?

   A. Technician A
   B. Technician B
   C. Both A and B
   D. Neither A nor B

8. When installing two fenders and a hood, Technician A installs the fenders first. In the same situation, Technician B installs the hood first. Who is correct?

   A. Technician A
   B. Technician B
   C. Both A and B
   D. Neither A nor B

9. When sectioning a B pillar, Technician A uses an offset butt joint. Technician B uses a butt joint with insert. Who is correct?

   A. Technician A
   B. Technician B
   C. Both A and B
   D. Neither A nor B

10. When replacing a panel, Technician A measures first and then installs the panel. Technician B installs the panel, checking by sight. Who is correct?

    A. Technician A
    B. Technician B
    C. Both A and B
    D. Neither A nor B

Chapter 13

Servicing Mechanical, Electrical, and Electronic Components

Job Sheet 13-1

Name_____ Date _____ Instructor Review _____

Remove and Replace a Radiator

Objective:

After completing this lab, the student should be able to remove a radiator, and fan motor, as well as mix the coolant and install a new radiator.

Equipment

Car in need of radiator repair
New radiator
Antifreeze/coolant
Water
Drip pan
Screwdrivers
Hand wrenches

Safety Equipment

Safety glasses

Procedure

Task Completed

1. Disconnect the battery. ❏

2. If the engine is hot, allow it to cool before working on the radiator. Find the drain valve at the bottom of the radiator. Place a drip pan under the valve. Open the valve and remove the radiator cap. ❏

3. Disconnect the overflow hose. If the car has an automatic transmission, disconnect the transmission cooler lines. Plug the ends of the lines. ❏

4. Loosen the clamps that hold the radiator hoses on. Twist the hoses and pull them off. Drain the hoses into the drip pan. ❏

5. Unplug the fan motor. Unbolt the radiator. ❏

6. If possible, pull the radiator and the fan motor out as one assembly. Unbolt the fan shroud from the radiator. In some cases, the fan shroud must be unbolted from the radiator while it is mounted on the car. Slide the fan out first; then pull the radiator out.   ❑

7. Check the condition of the radiator hoses. If they show bulges or deterioration, replace them. If possible, bolt the fan shroud to the new radiator. Install the new radiator. Plug the fan motor in.   ❑

8. Hook up the radiator hoses, transmission cooler lines and overflow hose.   ❑

9. Mix the antifreeze/coolant with water. Pour one-half gallon of antifreeze/coolant into a clean one gallon container. Add one-half gallon of water. This is a 50-50 mix.   ❑

10. Fill the radiator. Leave the radiator cap off. Start the car. When the engine warms up, the coolant level in the radiator will drop. Refill the radiator. Install the cap and fill the overflow tank. Check the transmission fluid level. Fill it if needed.   ❑

Job Sheet 13-2

Name_____ Date _____ Instructor Review _____

Recover and Reinstall A/C System Refrigerant

Objective

After studying the related textbook material and satisfactorily performing this task, the trainee should be able to recover and reinstall air conditioning system refrigerant.

Equipment

Eye and skin protection
Refrigeration recovery equipment
Vacuum pump
Gauge manifold
Refrigerant leak detector
Hand-held temperature gauge
Hand tools as needed
Temperature/pressure chart

Safety Equipment

Safety glasses

Procedure

Task Completed

1. Obtain a vehicle needing air conditioning service. ❏

   What is the make and model of the vehicle?

   Make _____

   Model _____

2. Determine what A/C system repairs must be performed. ❏

   Describe the needed repairs here.

   _____

   _____

   _____

3. Determine which type of refrigerant is being used in the A/C system. ❏

   R-12 _____ R-134a _____ R-22 _____

   Other _____

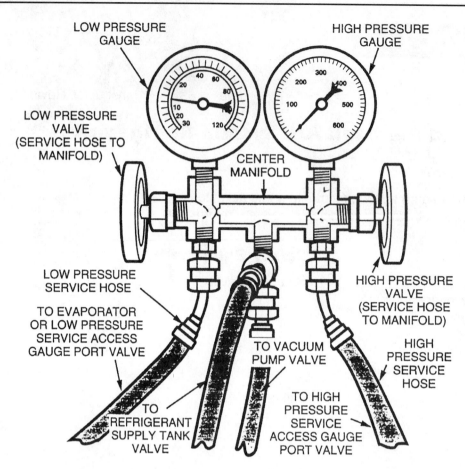

LOW PRESSURE
GAUGE

HIGH PRESSURE
GAUGE

LOW PRESSURE
VALVE
(SERVICE HOSE TO
MANIFOLD)

CENTER
MANIFOLD

LOW PRESSURE
SERVICE HOSE

HIGH PRESSURE
VALVE
(SERVICE HOSE
TO MANIFOLD)

TO EVAPORATOR
OR LOW PRESSURE
SERVICE ACCESS
GAUGE PORT VALVE

TO VACUUM
PUMP VALVE

HIGH
PRESSURE
SERVICE
HOSE

TO
REFRIGERANT
SUPPLY TANK
VALVE

TO HIGH
PRESSURE
SERVICE
ACCESS GAUGE
PORT VALVE

WARNING: Liquid refrigerant can cause severe damage to eyes and skin! Always wear proper eye and skin protection before beginning any service operations on the A/C system, or handling refrigerant containers.

**Task
Completed**

4. Locate the A/C system high and low side fittings and remove the protective caps. ❑

5. Obtain a refrigerant gauge manifold and all needed adapters (see figure above). ❑

What is the unit of pressure measurement? psi _____ kPa _____

What is the maximum reading on the high side gauge?_____

What is the maximum reading on the low side gauge? _____

Which gauge has a provision for reading vacuum?_____

What is the unit of vacuum measurement?

Inches of mercury (Hg) _____ Microns _____

6. Ensure that the gauge manifold valves are closed. ❑

7. Attach the high side gauge fitting to the high side of the A/C system. ❑

8. Attach the low side gauge fitting to the low side of the A/C system. ❑

9. Observe the gauges to determine whether the A/C system contains refrigerant. ❑

NOTE: If the A/C system contains no refrigerant, Steps 10 through 15 can only be simulated.

10. Obtain a refrigerant recovery unit. ❑

CAUTION: It is very important that you use a recovery unit designed to handle the same type of refrigerant as installed in the A/C system. Never mix different types of refrigerant.

Task Completed

11. Ensure that the refrigerant recovery unit is in operating condition: ❏

    The storage tank is not too full to accept additional refrigerant. _____

    The unit filters are not plugged. _____

    All electrical devices are operable. _____

    All switches are in the OFF position. _____

12. Attach the center connector of the gauge manifold to the refrigerant recovery unit. ❏

13. Open the hand valves on the gauge manifold. ❏

14. Start the refrigerant recovery unit pump. ❏

15. Allow the recovery unit to empty the A/C system. ❏

16. Close the hand valves on the gauge manifold. ❏

17. Carefully remove the necessary fittings and repair or replace the A/C system component(s) as needed. ❏

18. After repairs are completed, ensure that the A/C system has enough refrigerant oil, and add oil if necessary. ❏

19. Obtain a vacuum pump and attach it to the center hose of the gauge manifold. ❏

    What is the power source of the vacuum pump?

    Electric motor _____ Compressed air _____

20. Start the vacuum pump. ❏

21. Open the manifold hand valves and allow the pump to run for at least 30 minutes to evacuate all air and moisture from the A/C system. ❏

22. Observe the vacuum section of the low side gauge to ensure that vacuum has reached 29.9 inches of mercury, or about 150 to 200 microns. ❏

    NOTE: If the vacuum reading does not reach 29.9 inches of mercury or 150 to 200 microns, check for leaks or excessive moisture in the A/C system. Consult your instructor to obtain information on further A/C system service.

23. Close the gauge manifold hand valves. ❏

24. Turn the vacuum pump off. ❏

25. Monitor the low side gauge for at least 5 minutes, to determine whether the A/C system will hold vacuum. ❏

    CAUTION: If the A/C system does not hold vacuum, there is a leak in the system. Locate and correct the leak before proceeding.

    It is possible that the leak could be in the gauge manifold, and how would you correct it?

    _____

    _____

    If there is a leak in the system, where do you think you should start looking?

    _____

    _____

    What do you think should be done to correct a leak in the A/C system?

    _____

    _____

Task Completed

26. Determine how much refrigerant must be added to the A/C system to fully recharge it. ❑

    Write in the amount of refrigerant needed._____

    Is this amount given in pounds or kilograms? _____

27. Reattach the center hose of the gauge manifold to the refrigerant recovery unit. ❑

28. Turn the recovery unit on, and set it to deliver the amount of refrigerant determined in Procedure 26. ❑

29. Briefly loosen (crack) the center line at the gauge manifold to bleed any air from the line. ❑

30. Open the gauge manifold hand valves. ❑

31. Allow the recovery unit to recharge the A/C system. ❑

32. When the A/C system is completely recharged, close the gauge manifold hand valves. ❑

33. Turn the recovery unit off, and disconnect it from the gauge manifold. ❑

34. Leak check the A/C system. ❑

35. Place a hand-held temperature gauge in the center A/C outlet on the vehicle dashboard. ❑

36. Start the vehicle engine and turn on the A/C system. ❑

37. Monitor the A/C system for proper operation: ❑

    High side pressure _____

    Low side pressure _____

    Discharge air temperature _____

    NOTE: High and low side pressures, and discharge air temperatures, vary greatly with changes in ambient (outside) air temperature and humidity. Consult a temperature/pressure chart for the type of refrigerant being used in the A/C system.

38. Correct any problems as necessary. ❑

39. Remove the gauge manifold from the A/C system. ❑

40. Dispose of old parts and scrap. ❑

41. Return all tools to storage. ❑

42. Clean the work area. ❑

Job Questions

1. How long did it take to:

   Remove the refrigerant from the A/C system?_____

   Evacuate the system? _____

   Recharge the system? _____

2. Exactly what was done to repair the A/C system?

   _____

   _____

3. Were the repairs the same as what you expected at the beginning of the job (Procedure 2)?
   Yes _____ No _____ If not, what were the differences?

   _____

   _____

4. Were any of the following problems experienced during A/C system servicing?
   Leaks _____ If so, where were they located? _____
   Noises when operating _____ Vibrations _____
   Evaporator freeze-up _____ Incorrect pressures _____
   Insufficient cooling _____
   If the answer to any of the above was yes, what was done to correct the problem?

   _____

   _____

   _____

   _____

   _____

   _____

5. Was the problem in the refrigeration part of the A/C system, or some other area? Explain:

   _____

   _____

   _____

   _____

   _____

   _____

Job Sheet 13-3

Name_____ Date _____ Instructor Review _____

Rack and Pinion Replacement

Objective

After completing this lab, the student should be able to replace a rack and pinion and tie rod ends.

Equipment

Car with rack and pinion steering
Tie rod and socket
Service manual
Fork

Safety Equipment

Safety glasses

Procedure

Torque all bolts to specifications!

Task Completed

1. Obtain a service manual for the type of vehicle you are working on. Read over the section on tie rods and rack and pinion. ❏

2. Raise the vehicle and support it on jack stands. Remove the front wheels. ❏

3. Remove the Cotter pin from the nut that bolts the tie rod to the steering knuckle. Remove the nut. ❏

4. Disconnect the tie rod from the knuckle with a fork. Be careful not to damage the boot. ❏

5. Unbolt the outer tie rod. In some cases, a special socket is needed. ❏

6. The rack may be bolted to the cowl or the engine cradle. Remove any hoses that are in the way. ❏

7. Disconnect the steering linkage. Slide back the boot and loosen the bolt. Slide the linkage out. ❏

8. Unbolt the rack and remove it. ❏

9. To reassemble, install the rack on the cowl or engine cradle. Slide the steering linkage into place and bolt it in. Install the outer tie rods. ❏

10. Reconnect the outer tie rod ends to the steering knuckle. Replace the wheel. A front end alignment may be needed. ❏

Job Sheet 13-4

Name_____ Date _____ Instructor Review _____

CV Joint Boot Replacement

Objective

After completing this lab, the student should be able to remove a front wheel drive half shaft and remove/replace/install the CV joint boot.

Equipment

Front wheel drive vehicle
Hub puller
Sockets
Service manual
Rachet
Breaker bar

Safety Equipment

Safety glasses

Procedure

Task Completed

1. Obtain a service manual for the type of vehicle you have. Read the procedures. ❏

2. Remove the wheel cover and hub cover. Loosen the hub nut with a socket and breaker bar. Raise the car and support it on jack stands. ❏

3. Remove the wheel. Unscrew the hub nut. Remove the brake line retainer from the suspension. Support the brake caliper. Disconnect the ball joint. ❏

4. Pull out on the strut; pull in on the half shaft. This should separate the outboard CV joint and the suspension. A hub puller can be used if there is trouble. ❏

5. Pull out the inboard CV joint. Do not pull on the half shaft. It could break the joint. ❏

6. Place the half shaft in a soft-jawed vise. Cut off the boot clamp. Scribe the boot location on the shaft. Slide the boot back up the shaft. Remove the circlip and pull the joint from the shaft. Slide the boot off. ❏

7. Clean the shaft. Put the new boot onto the shaft. ❏

8. Install the joint. Used a new circlip. Pack all of the grease included with the boot into the boot and joint. ❏

9. Slide the new boot over the joint. Align with the scribed marks. Purge the air. Install the new clamps. ❏

10. Slice the half shaft into the transaxle. Pull the suspension out and put over the outboard joint. Install the ball joint, brake hose retainer, hub nut, and wheel. Lower the car and torque the hub nut. A front end alignment may be needed. ❏

Job Sheet 13-5

Name_____ Date _____ Instructor Review _____

McPherson Strut Replacement

Objective

After completing this lab, the student should be able to remove and replace a McPherson strut on a vehicle.

Equipment

Car with McPherson strut
McPherson strut spray compressor
Service manual
Lift

Safety Equipment

Safety glasses

Procedure

Task Completed

1. Obtain a service manual for the type of vehicle you are working on. Read over the procedure. Also read the strut spring compressor operation manual. ❏

2. Mark the location of the strut bolts on the shock tower. This will aid in alignment. ❏

3. Raise the car on a lift. Remove the wheel. ❏

4. Remove the brake liner retainer. Remove the strut to the steering knuckle bolts. ❏

5. Support the steering knuckle with wire. Loosen the strut bolts on the shock tower. ❏

6. Remove the strut assembly. Mount the unit in a strut spring compressor. Tighten the compressor. ❏

7. Loosen the retaining nut. Remove the strut from the spring. You may have to let tension off of the spring. ❏

8. Slide the new strut into the spring. Tighten the retaining nut. ❏

9. Install the new assembly into the shock tower. Bolt the steering knuckle to the strut. Align the strut bolts with the marks on the shock tower. Install the brake line retainer. ❏

10. Install the wheel. Lower the car. The vehicle may need a front-end alignment. ❏

Job Sheet 13-6

Name_____ Date _____ Instructor Review _____

Dissect Parallelogram Steering System

Objective

After completing this lab, the student should be able to test, remove, and replace parallelogram steering components.

Equipment

Vehicle with parallelogram steering
Sockets—rachet
Torque wrench
Pitman arm puller
Hammer
Tie rod end fork
Power steering fluid
Cotter pins
Line wrenches
Side cutters
Drain pan

Safety Equipment

Safety glasses

Procedure

Task Completed

1. Raise the vehicle and place the jack stands under the frame. Do not get under the vehicle until it is properly mounted on jack stands. Make a labeled drawing of the steering system parts in the space below.   ❏

2. Grasp and twist the tie rods, center link, idler area and Pitman arm. Any play means that there is a problem. Collision damage is indicated by bends or a change in the rust pattern on the part. List the problem components.   ❑

_____

_____

_____

_____

3. Start the center link removal at a tie rod end. Locate the Cotter pin on the nut. Cut off the legs of the Cotter pin and pull it out. Slip a tie rod end fork into the joint between the link and the tie rod end. Be careful not to damage the boot. A damaged boot must be replaced. Hit the fork with a hammer to drive the components apart.   ❑

4. Remove the center link from the other tie rod end, idler arm and pitman arm all in the same manner.   ❑

5. Remove the tie rod ends from the steering knuckle by pulling out the Cotter pin and unbolting the nut. You can loosen the tie rod end by striking the hammer on the steering knuckle joint. You can also use the fork.   ❑

6. Unbolt the idler arm from the frame mounts. Take off the bolt holding the pitman arm to the steering gear box. Remove the Pitman arm with a puller. Fit the puller around the Pitman arm and tighten the bolt. It will take considerable force to remove the arm.   ❑

7. If the vehicle has power steering, loosen the hydraulic line nuts at the steering gear box. Put a drain pan under the vehicle. Disconnect the steering shaft from the steering box. Unbolt the steering box from the frame. Be careful—it is heavy.   ❑

8. Obtain any replacement parts. Check the service manual for proper torque on all bolts. Begin the reassembly by bolting and torquing the steering box in place. Connect the steering shaft. Hook up the power steering hydraulic lines.   ❑

9. Reconnect all of the linkages and tie rods by sliding the joints together, torquing the nut and replacing the cotter pins.   ❑

10. Fill the power steering reservoir. Start the vehicle. Bleed the air out of the power steering by turning the steering wheel from lock to lock several times. The vehicle now needs a front-end alignment.   ❑

Job Sheet 13-7

Name_____ Date _____ Instructor Review _____

Rear Axle Repair

Objective

After completing this lab, the student should be able to remove and replace a rear wheel drive axle.

Equipment

Rear wheel drive vehicle
Drain pan
Service manual
Sockets—rachet

Safety Equipment

Safety glasses

Procedure

Task Completed

1. Obtain a service manual for the vehicle you are working on. Consult the manual for the proper procedure. ❏

2. Place a floor jack under the differential. Raise the vehicle. Place jack stands under the axle housing. Lower the car onto the jack stands. Do not get under the car until it is safely supported by jack stands. ❏

3. To check the axle for damage, spin the wheel. It is easier to see the wobble if you place a pencil or pointer on a stand beside the wheel. See if the wheel moves in and out from the pointer. Remove the wheel and check it again. If there is wobble, the axle is bent. If there isn't any wobble, only the wheel is bent. ❏

4. Place a drain pan under the differential. If the rear end has a drain plug, remove the plug. Unbolt the cover. ❏

5. Remove the wheel and the brake drum. ❏

6. Check the service manual for the proper procedure. It may be possible to unbolt the axle from the backing plate and slide the axle out. The other way is to remove the retaining bolt inside the differential, push in on the axle and then pull out a C clip. The axle will now slide out. ❏

7. Do not move the differential gears when the axle is out. If they do get moved, they must be realigned before the axle is put back in. ❏

8. Slide the new axle into place. Rebolt or replace the C clip and bolt. Reinstall the differential cover, brake drum and wheel. ❏

9. Check for wobble by spinning the wheel. Take the car off of the jack stands. ❏

10. Fill the differential with the proper grade of oil. ❏

Job Sheet 13-8

Name_____ Date _____ Instructor Review _____

Brakes

Objective

After completing this lab, the student should be able to manually bleed the brakes after a brake hose has been replaced.

Equipment

Car
Wrench
Brake fluid
Jar
Service manual
Two people
Hose

Safety Equipment

Safety glasses

Procedure

Task Completed

1. Obtain a service manual for the vehicle you are working on. Read over the procedure for brake bleeding. ❏

2. Locate the bleeder valve on the brake. Attach a hose to the bleeder valve. On power brakes, remove the vacuum line from the power unit. Unplug the unit. ❏

3. Open the cap on the master cylinder. Pour brake fluid from a sealed container into the master cylinder. The master cylinder must not go dry during the bleeding. Pour the brake fluid into the jar. ❏

4. Position the jar so that the hose is in the fluid. ❏

5. Have the technician in the car pump the brake pedal. Then have him hold down the pedal. ❏

6. Have the outside technician open the bleeder valve. When the fluid and bubbles stop flowing, close the valve. ❏

7. The technician inside the car should slowly release the brake pedal. ❏

8. The inside technician will again pump the brake pedal and hold it down. The outside technician will then open the bleeder valve. ❏

9. When the fluid is clear and there are no bubbles, the bleeding is complete. Repeat this process until you reach this stage. ❏

10. Fill the master cylinder. ❏

Job Sheet 13-9

Name_____ Date _____ Instructor Review _____

Align Suspension and Steering Components

Objective

After studying the related textbook material and satisfactorily performing this task, the trainee should be able to align suspension and steering components.

Equipment

Alignment rack and related equipment
Alignment adjusting tools
Hand and power tools as needed

Safety Equipment

Safety glasses

Task Completed

Procedure

NOTE: After a collision, it is often necessary to align the vehicle to prevent tire wear and handling problems. Simply replacing damaged parts and setting the vehicle toe is not sufficient. Every step of the following process should be performed.

1. Obtain a vehicle in need of suspension and steering component alignment. The vehicle is a: ❑

   Make _____

   Model _____

   Year _____

2. Drive the vehicle onto a suitable alignment rack. ❑

   NOTE: To ensure accurate alignment readings, the vehicle must be driven as straight as possible onto the alignment rack.

3. Check for worn or damaged suspension or steering components. ❑

   CAUTION: The vehicle cannot be aligned if any suspension or steering part is bent or worn excessively. Worn or bent parts must be replaced before proceeding with the alignment.

   What type of suspension does this vehicle have?_____

   _____

   Front (struts, upper and lower control arms, etc.)

   _____

   _____

   Rear (Leaf springs, coil springs, struts, etc.)

   _____

   _____

   Is either axle a solid axle?

   Front: Yes _____ No _____

   Rear: Yes _____ No _____

4. Obtain the correct alignment specifications for the vehicle (see figure below).

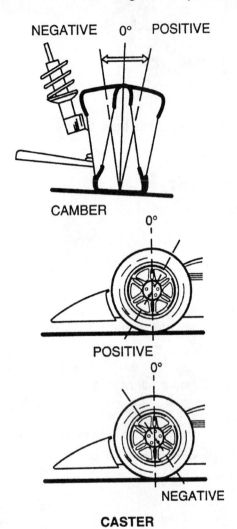

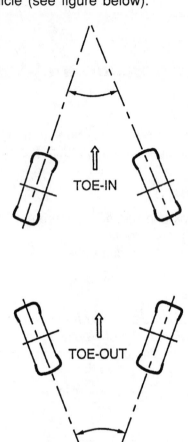

Does this vehicle require a 2-wheel or 4-wheel alignment?

2 wheel _____ 4 wheel _____

5. Check the tire pressure, and ensure that all tires match by size and type.   ❏

Write the following information about the tires:

Rim size _____

Tire size _____

Manufacturer _____

Radial _____ Conventional _____

Air pressure in psi _____

6. Check the vehicle ride height.   ❏

7. Attach alignment equipment to the vehicle wheels according to the equipment
    manufacturer's instructions.   ❏

8. Adjust for wheel rim runout according to the equipment manufacturer's instructions.   ❏

Task Completed

9. Check vehicle front wheel camber according to the equipment manufacturer's instructions. ❑

10. Record the front camber for future reference. ❑

    Front camber specifications _____

    Actual front camber reading _____

11. Check vehicle front wheel caster according to the equipment manufacturer's instructions. ❑

12. Record the front caster for future reference. ❑

    Front caster specifications _____

    Actual front caster reading _____

13. Check vehicle front wheel toe according to the equipment manufacturer's instructions. ❑

14. Record the front toe for future reference. ❑

    Front toe specifications _____

    Actual front toe reading _____

15. If necessary, check and record the rear camber. ❑

    Rear camber specifications _____

    Actual rear camber reading _____

16. If necessary, check and record the rear toe. ❑

    Rear toe specifications _____

    Actual rear toe reading _____

17. Obtain the appropriate alignment service literature and determine the proper alignment adjustment methods. ❑

    NOTE: This information can be found in factory service manuals, general manuals such as Motor *or* Chilton's, *or special alignment specification books.*

    Explain how the alignment adjustments are made (by turning eccentric cams, installing shims, loosening bolts and pulling on the wheel, turning threaded rods, etc.). If no adjustment is provided, write "none."

    Rear camber _____

    Rear toe _____

    Front camber _____

    Front caster _____

    Front toe _____

18. Adjust the rear camber as needed. ❑

19. Adjust the rear toe as needed. ❑

20. Adjust the front camber. ❑

21. Recheck the caster. ❑

22. Adjust caster as needed. ❑

23. Ensure that adjusting the caster has not affected front camber readings. ❑

24. Repeat Steps 20 through 23 as needed to correct the front camber and caster. ❑

25. When front camber and caster are correct, center the steering wheel. ❑

26. Adjust the front toe. ❑

Task Completed

27. Re-center the steering wheel and recheck the front toe.   ❏

28. Readjust the toe to center the wheel, if needed.   ❏

29. Remove the alignment equipment from the wheel rims.   ❏

30. Drive the vehicle from the alignment rack.   ❏

31. Drive the vehicle and ensure that it is aligned correctly: ❏

   Vehicle does not pull to the left or right on a flat road _____

   Vehicle does not wander excessively _____

   Steering wheel is straight when driving straight forward _____

32. Return all tools to storage.   ❏

33. Clean the work area.   ❏

Job Questions

1. What problems did you encounter when making the alignment adjustments (frozen fasteners, hard-to-move adjusters, no more adjustment left, etc.)?

   _____

   _____

2. What did you do to make sure that the alignment was done correctly?

   _____

   _____

3. Was it necessary to re-center the steering wheel after making the first front toe adjustment?

   Yes _____ No _____

   Why is centering the steering wheel important?

   _____

   _____

4. Why is it important to adjust the rear suspension on front-wheel drive vehicles?

   _____

   _____

5. What special tools were required to align the vehicle?

   _____

   _____

6. Were any special parts (such as adjustable cam kits or rear wheel shims) needed to align the vehicle?

   _____

   _____

Job Sheet 13-10

Name_____ Date _____ Instructor Review _____

Drive Train Removal

Objective

After completing this lab, the student should be able to remove a drive train from a front wheel drive, engine cradle equipped vehicle.

Equipment

Car with an engine cradle
Engine dolly
Lift
Hand tools

Safety Equipment

Safety glasses

Procedure

Task Completed

1. Drain the A/C system. This must be done by a licensed operator. ❑

2. Drain the radiator. Disconnect the radiator hoses from the engine. Disconnect and unplug the A/C lines. ❑

3. Unbolt the main electrical connection at the cowl. Disconnect the fuel line and battery. ❑

4. Raise the car on a lift. Disconnect the following: ❑

   Exhaust pipe at the engine

   Steering linkage at the rack and pinion

   Brake lines at caliper

5. Place the engine dolly under the engine cradle. Lower the car onto the dolly. ❑

6. Unbolt the four cradle bolts. ❑

7. Unbolt the nuts holding the strut to the shock tower. ❑

8. Raise the car slowly. Watch for any lines that have not been disconnected. ❑

9. Wheel the dolly out from underneath the car. ❑

10. To reinstall, reverse the disassembly sequence. ❑

Job Sheet 13-11

Name_____ Date _____ Instructor Review _____

Electrical System

Objective

After completing this lab, the student should be able to change a battery, splice a wire, and make simple electrical tests.

Equipment

Car with power windows and
　power door locks
Automotive electrical wires
Battery charger
Rosin core solder
Soldering gun
Battery
Heat gun
Test light
Jumper wires

Safety Equipment

Safety glasses

Procedure

Task Completed

1. Remove the trim panel from a rear door. Pull off the protective plastic shield. Reconnect the switches for the window and the lock. Locate the power window regulator and the power door lock solenoid.　❑

2. Unplug the regulator and the solenoid. Use a test light on the circuits. Connect the ground to the bare metal on the door. Probe each of the plugs with the test light. Record the results below.　❑

_____

_____

_____

3. Turn the key so the car's electrical system is on. Again, probe the plugs and record the results below.　❑

_____

_____

_____

4. Operate the window and lock switches while probing the plug. Record the results.　❑

_____

_____

_____

5. Attach the jumper wires to the spare battery. Touch the wires to the terminals on the regulator and solenoid. Record the results.   ❏

_____

_____

_____

6. Plug in the battery charger. Adjust it to 12V, low charge. Hook up jumper wires to the clamps. Touch the jumper wires to the terminals on the regulator and solenoid. Record the results.   ❏

_____

_____

_____

7. Turn the ignition off and reconnect the regulator and solenoid. Disconnect the window switch; then turn the ignition back on. Use a jumper wire to bypass the switch. Record the results.   ❏

_____

_____

_____

8. Plug in the soldering gun and allow it to warm up. Splice wires together by first slipping a shrink tube over one of the wires. Now strip off one inch of insulation from each wire end. Twist the bare copper wires together. Heat the twisted wires with the soldering gun. Touch the rosin core solder to the twisted wires. The heat on the wires should melt the solder. Cover the entire joint. After the solder has hardened, slide the shrink tube over the joint. Use a heat gun to contract the tube.   ❏

9. Your instructor will demonstrate how to properly charge the battery on a dead vehicle. Summarize the procedure in the space below.   ❏

_____

_____

_____

Review Questions

Name_____ Date _____·_____ Instructor Review _____

1. The drive train should be removed whenever a frame rail is sectioned.

   A. True
   B. False

2. A CV joint boot is torn. Technician A states the boot must be replaced. Technician B believes the boot and the joint must be replaced. Who is correct?

   A. Technician A
   B. Technician B
   C. Both A and B
   D. Neither A nor B

3. When removing a drive train from a vehicle, Technician A raises the car with a jack and places it on jack stands. Technician B raises the car with a lift. Who is correct?

   A. Technician A
   B. Technician B
   C. Both A and B
   D. Neither A nor B

4. _____ are found at the outer end of the control arms and allow the steering knuckles to turn.

5. Misalignment of the rack and pinion causes bump steer.

   A. True
   B. False

6. _____ causes the wheel to wobble sideways as it rotates.

7. The included angle is the SAI plus camber.

   A. True
   B. False

8. Technician A states brake fluid must be kept in a sealed container. Technician B believes water contaminated brake fluid can lead to loss of braking ability. Who is correct?

   A. Technician A
   B. Technician B
   C. Both A and B
   D. Neither A nor B

9. The exansion valve converts high pressure liquid to low pressure liquid.

   A. True
   B. False

10. If you test an open circuit with a DVOM, you will get a reading of 1.

    A. True
    B. False

Chapter 14

Repairing Auto Plastics

Shop Assignment 14-1

Name_____ Date _____ Instructor Review _____

Plastic ID Lab

	Name	Thermoplastic/ Thermoset	Repair Method
1. PUR	_____	_____	_____
2. ABS	_____	_____	_____
3. PP	_____	_____	_____
4. TPO	_____	_____	_____
5. E/P	_____	_____	_____
6. UP	_____	_____	_____
7. SMC	_____	_____	_____
8. RRIM	_____	_____	_____
9. PPO	_____	_____	_____
10. PE	_____	_____	_____
11. PA	_____	_____	_____
12. ABS + PC	_____	_____	_____
13. PC	_____	_____	_____
14. TPR	_____	_____	_____
15. ABS + PVC	_____	_____	_____

Job Sheet 14-1

Name_____ Date _____ Instructor Review

Urethane Flexible Bumper Repairs

Objective

After completing this lab, the student should be able to repair scratches and tears in urethane bumpers.

Equipment

Urethane bumper
Knife
Flexible primer
80, 220 and 400 grit paper
Flexible repair material
Sanding block
Fiberglass cloth
Duct tape
Plastic cleaner
Body filler spreader

Safety Equipment

Safety glasses
Dust respirator
Leather gloves

Procedure

Task Completed

1. Wash the bumper with soap and water. Clean with a plastic cleaner. Use a knife to make a six-inch scratch in the bumper. Be sure to scratch deep into the urethane.   ❏

2. Block sand the scratch with 220 grit paper. Sand until $\frac{1}{2}$" of each paint layer is exposed. Complete the featheredge by sanding with 400 grit paper. Sand until one inch of each paint layer is exposed.   ❏

3. Mix the flexible repair material and apply to the scratch. Do not get any of the material on unsanded areas. Overfill and allow it to cure.   ❏

4. Sand the hardened flexible repair material with 80 grit paper to remove roughness. Complete sanding with 220 grit paper, followed by 400 grit paper.   ❏

5. Spray on a flexible primer. Laquer-based aerosol primer may be used, or you can mix urethane primer with a flex agent.   ❏

6. Use a knife to make a four inch cut in the bumper. This will simulate a tear.   ❏

7. Clean and sand the back side of the rear with 80 grit paper. Sand three inches to either side of the cut. Bevel and feather edge the front side of the cut with 80 grit paper.   ❏

8. Mix flexible repair material. Cut out two pieces of 6" x 2" fiberglass cloth to serve as a reinforcement. Carefully align the edges of the cut. Use duct tape on the front side to maintain alignment. Apply a coat of flexible repair material to the back side of the repair area. Stay within the sanded area. Lay a piece of fiberglass cloth on the flexible repair material. Work this piece into the flexible repair material with the body filler spreader. Apply a final layer of flexible repair material over the cloth.   ❏

9. After the flexible repair material on the back side has hardened, remove the duct tape from the front side and overfill the beveled cut with flexible repair material. Allow this to harden.   ❏

10. Sand the front side with 80 grit paper. Then feather edge with 220 grit paper followed by 400 grit paper. Apply a flexible primer.   ❏

Job Sheet 14-2

Name_____ Date _____ Instructor Review _____

Shrink and Shape Urethane

Objective

After completing this lab, the student should be able to shrink and shape urethane.

Equipment

Damaged urethane bumper
Heat gun
Ice or wet rag
Wooden paint stick

Safety Equipment

Safety glasses

Procedure

Task Completed

Shrink

1. Stretch can be recognized by a bulging or swollen area. Locate a stretched area on a bumper. ❏

2. Use a heat gun set on high heat to warm up the center of the swollen area. The plastic will heat rapidly, so be careful. ❏

3. When the plastic has heated up, rapidly cool it with a wet rag or ice. ❏

4. Repeat this process with the remaining swollen areas. ❏

Shape

5. Collision damaged bumpers are often bent out of shape. Heat can be used to reshape them. Obtain a collision damaged urethane bumper. ❏

6. Examine the damage. Decide where the plastic is damaged and where it needs to be moved. ❏

7. Warm the first area to be moved with a heat gun set on high. When the plastic is hot to the touch, it can be moved into its proper location with a paint stick. ❏

8. When the damaged area is in the right location, rapidly cool the area with a wet rag or ice. ❏

9. Repeat the procedure on other damaged areas. ❏

Job Sheet 14-3

Name_____ Date _____ Instructor Review _____

SMC Repairs

Objective

After completion of this lab, the student should know how to repair SMC panels.

Equipment

SMC Panel
Rigid repair material filler
Rigid repair material adhesive
80, 220 and 400 sand paper
Sanding block
Body filler spreader
Hammer
Duct tape
Fiberglass cloth
Cut off tool
Plastic cleaner

Safety Equipment

Safety glasses
Dust respirator
Leather gloves

Procedure

Scratch

Task Completed

1. Clean the SMC panel with a plastic cleaner. Make a six-inch scratch deep into the plastic.   ❑

2. Sand the area around the scratch with 80 grit paper. Mix rigid repair material filler. Overfill the scratch with the filler. Allow to cure.   ❑

3. Sand the filler with 80 grit paper to level. Feather edge paint with 220 grit paper, followed by 400 grit paper.   ❑

Break

4. Use a hammer to break the plastic. Clean and sand the back side of the panel with 80 grit paper. Sand an area at least three inches to either side of the break. Align the broken area with duct tape on the front side.   ❑

5. Mix rigid repair material adhesive. Cut out three pieces of fiberglass cloth the same size as the repair area. Apply a layer of adhesive with a body filler spreader. Put a fiberglass piece over the adhesive. Push it into place with the spreader. Lay down another coat of adhesive, then another piece of fiberglass. Apply more adhesive, followed by the last piece of fiberglass. Cover the top piece with adhesive. Press the adhesive into the fiberglass with the spreader. Allow to cure.   ❑   ❑

6. Remove the duct tape from the front side. Sand off the paint with 80 grit paper. Mix up rigid repair material filler and overfill the low areas.   ❑

7. When the filler has dried, sand with 80 grit paper. Featheredge the paint with 200 grit paper, followed by 400 grit paper.   ❏

Splice

8. Cut a 4" x 2" rectangle out of the SMC panel with a cut off tool. Cut out two 1" x 5" backers from a scrap piece of SMC. Clean and sand (with 80 grit paper) the back side of the hole and the backers. Mix rigid repair material adhesive. Apply to the long sides of the rectangle. Place the backers in the adhesive. Overlap the hole by one-half inch. Allow the proper cure time.   ❏

9. Clean and sand both sides of the cut out rectangle. Mix up the rigid repair material adhesive and spread a coat on the overlapped portion of the backers. Place the cut out rectangle on the backers. Allow this to cure.   ❏

10. Clean, sand with 80 grit paper, and bevel the area around the hole. Mix rigid repair material filler and overfill the gaps between the hole and the cut out piece. Allow time to cure. Sand the filler with 80 grit paper. Featheredge with 220 grit paper, followed by 400 grit paper.   ❏

Job Sheet 14-4

Name_____ Date _____ Instructor Review _____

Fiberglass Reinforced Plastic Repairs

Objective

After completing this lab, the student should be able to repair fiberglass reinforced plastic.

Equipment

FRP header panel
Body filler
Fiberglass resin
Fiberglass mat
80, 220 and 400 grit sandpaper
Plastic cleaner
Sanding block
Knife
Hammer
Body filler spreader
Rubber gloves
Duct tape

Safety Equipment

Safety glasses
Dust respirator
Leather gloves

Procedure

Task Completed

Scratch

1. Clean the panel with plastic cleaner. Use the knife to make a six-inch scratch into the fiberglass.   ❏

2. Sand on the scratch with 80 grit paper on the sanding block. Mix and apply body filler to overfill the scratch.   ❏

3. After the body filler has cured, sand with 80 grit paper on the block. Featheredge with 200 or 400 grit paper.   ❏

Break Two-sided Repair

4. Break the header panel by hitting it with a hammer. Clean with plastic cleaner. Sand the back side of the panel with 80 grit paper. Sand it at least three inches on each side of the break. Align the repair area with duct tape on the front side.   ❏

5. Mix up fiberglass resin and hardener. Cut out three pieces of fiberglass cloth that are the same size as the sanded area. Use rubber gloves as you dip the cloth in the resin. Apply the cloth to the sanded area. Smooth with a body filler spreader. Put the remaining pieces on in the same manner. A heat lamp may be used to speed the dry time. Allow to cure.   ❏

6. Remove the duct tape. Sand the front side with 80 grit paper until it is smooth.   ❏

7. Mix up the body filler. Spread it on the front side to fill any remaining cracks. Sand the cured body filler with 80 grit paper. Then featheredge with 200 grit paper, followed by 400 grit paper.   ❏

One-sided Repair

8. Break the header panel by hitting it with a hammer. Align the broken edges. If the fiberglass strands prevent alignment, use a grinder with a 24 grit disk to remove the strands. Bevel the broken area with the grinder. Do not make a hole through the fiberglass. If a hole is made, it is best to repair that type of damage using the two-sided repair method.   ❏

9. Mix resin and hardener. Cut out three pieces of fiberglass cloth that will be the same size as the repair area. Dip the fiberglass in the mixed resin. Use rubber gloves to apply one piece at a time to the area. Smooth with a body filler spreader. Allow proper cure time.   ❏

10. After the repair has cured, sand with 80 grit paper. If the repair area is difficult to sand, a grinder with 24 grit paper may be used. This will rapidly remove the repaired fiberglass, so be careful. Complete the sanding with 220 and 400 grit paper.   ❏

Job Sheet 14-5

Name_____ Date _____ Instructor Review _____

Plastic Welding

Objective

After completing this lab, the student should be able to weld ABS, PP and PE parts.

Equipment

Airless welder
ABS, PP and PE parts
Welding rod
Plastic cleaner
Duct tape
Grinder
Hacksaw

Safety Equipment

Safety glasses

Procedure

Task Completed

ABS

1. If the ABS part is not broken, snap it in two to obtain a broken edge for repair. Clean the part with soap and water. Then use a plastic cleaner. Align the front side of the part with duct tape. Use a slow speed grinder on the back side to taper the break.   ❑

2. Allow the welder to heat up to the proper temperature. Clean and sand an area on the back side of the panel. Put an ABS rod on the sanded spot and use the shoe of the welder to melt it. Remove the welder shoe and allow it to cool. If the rod sticks to the part, the ABS rod can be used for welding. If the rod does not stick, find a hidden area of the part to shave off slivers.   ❑

3. Melt the filler material (rod or slivers) into the joint. Move the shoe slowly for good penetration.   ❑

4. Use the edge of the shoe to make a series perpendicular grooves in the weld. These will mix the filler and the base material.   ❑

5. Smooth out the rough grooves with the flat part of the shoe.   ❑

6. Remove the duct tape from the front side. Use a slow grinder to taper the joint. You need to grind enough to reach the weld.   ❑

7. Again, melt in filler and make grooves.   ❑

8. Smooth the grooves with the shoe.   ❑

9. Additional smoothing may be done by shaving with a razor blade or light sanding with 80 grit paper.   ❑

PP

10. If the part is not broken, use a hacksaw or cut off tool to make a cut in the part.   ❑

11. Clean the part with soap and water. Next clean it with a plastic cleaner. Align the damaged edges with duct tape.   ❑

12. Taper the damaged edge on the back side with a slow speed grinder. Drill $1/8$" holes into the tapered edge. Place these holes every $3/8$" along both tapered edges.   ❑

13. Test by the weld rod by melting the rod on a cleaned and sanded area. Weld with a compatable weld rod. Smooth the weld with the shoe.   ❑

14. Remove the tape. If this is a visible part, you can sand, apply adhesion promoter, followed by flexible filler.   ❑

PE

15. If the PE part has no damage, cut the part with a hacksaw or cut off tool.   ❑

16. Clean the part with soap and water. Then clean it with a plastic cleaner. Align the damaged edges with duct tape.   ❑

17. Use a slow speed grinder to taper the damaged edges.   ❑

18. Test the weld rod by melting the rod onto a cleaned and sanded area of the part. If the rod does not stick, shave off slivers of the part from an inconspicuous area. Weld with a PE compatible rod or slivers.   ❑

19. Smooth the weld by cutting with a razor blade.   ❑

Job Sheet 14-6

Name_____ Date _____ Instructor Review _____

RRIM Repairs

Objective

After completing this lab, the student should be able to repair RRIM.

Equipment

RRIM panel
Plastic cleaner
80, 220 and 400 grit paper
Body filler spreader
Rigid repair material—filler
Knife
Hacksaw or cut off tool
Rigid repair material—adhesive complete
Fiberglass cloth

Safety Equipment

Safety glasses
Dust respirator
Leather gloves

Procedure

Task Completed

Scratch

1. Wash the part with soap and water, Clean with a plastic cleaner. Use a knife to make a six-inch scratch in the plastic. ❑

2. Sand the area around the scratch with 80 grit paper. Bevel the cut with 80 grit paper. Mix rigid repair material filler. Overfill the scratch. Allow cure time. ❑

3. Sand the filler with 80 grit paper. Featheredge the paint with 220 grit paper, followed by 400 grit paper. ❑

Break

4. Use a hacksaw or cut off tool to make a six-inch cut in the part. Make an additional three-inch cut perpendicular to the first cut. This is to simulate how this type of plastic breaks. ❑

5. Clean the front and back side of the repair area with soap and water. Then use a plastic cleaner. Align the front side of the repair with duct tape. ❑

6. Sand the back side of the repair with 80 grit paper. Sand at least two inches around the break. ❑

7. Cut out two pieces of fiberglass cloth the same size as the repair area. Mix rigid repair material—adhesive. ❑

8. Spread a layer of adhesive on the repair area. Lay a piece of fiberglass cloth over the adhesive. Push the cloth in with a body filler spreader. Apply more adhesive and put on the last piece of fiberglass. Allow cure time. ❑

9. Remove the duct tape on the front side. Bevel the cut with 80 grit paper. Mix rigid repair material—filler. Overfill the cut. Allow cure time. ❑

10. Sand filler with 80 grit paper. Featheredge the paint with 220 grit paper, followed by 400 grit paper. ❑

Job Sheet 14-7

Name_____ Date _____ Instructor Review _____

PC Repairs

Objective

After completing this lab, the student should be able to make bonding repairs on PC, lexan or nascote parts.

Equipment

PC bumper
Knife or awl
Flexible repair material
Duct tape
Hacksaw or cut off tool
Fiberglass cloth
Plastic cleaner

Safety Equipment

Safety glasses
Dust respirator
Leather gloves

Procedure

Task Completed

1. Wash the part with soap and water. Then use a plastic cleaner. Repairs can be made on the sides, slides and cosmetic repairs on the front. Repairs on the boxed reinforcement are not recommended. ❏

Cosmetic Scratch

2. If the part is not scratched, use a knife or awl to gouge the part. Taper the scratch with 80 grit paper. ❏

3. Overfill the scratch with flexible repair material. Allow cure time. Sand with 80 grit paper. Then feather edge with 200 grit paper, followed by 400 grit paper. ❏

Side

4. If the part is not broken, use a hacksaw or cut off tool to damage the part. Clean the back side of the repair area with soap and water. Then use a plastic cleaner. Align the front side with duct tape. ❏

5. Sand an area two inches on either side of the break with 80 grit paper. Cut out two pieces of fiberglass cloth large enough to cover the repair area. ❏

6. Mix flexible repair material. Put a layer of material on the sanded area. Place a piece of fiberglass on the material. Work the cloth into the material with a body filler spreader. Apply another layer of material followed with another piece of cloth. Work the cloth into the material. Put a final coat of material over the cloth. Allow to cure. ❏

7. Remove the tape from the front side. Bevel the cut area and sand about one inch on either side of the cut with 80 grit paper. ❏

8. Overfill the cut with flexible repair material. Then sand with 80 grit paper, followed with 220 grit paper. Finish with 400 grit paper. ❏

Slides

9. Slides can be repaired by bonding. If the slide is attached to the part, break it off. Clean and sand both surfaces. Apply a layer of flexible repair material to the slide. ❏

10. Properly align the slide on the bumper. Hold in place with duct tape. Allow to cure and check alignment by placing it on the car. ❏

Job Sheet 14-8

Name_____ Date _____ Instructor Review _____

Olefin Containing Plastic Repair

Objective

After completing this lab, the student should be able to determine which parts contain olefin and how to make bonding repairs on them.

Equipment

Olefin part
Plastic cleaner
Hacksaw or cut off tool
Body filler spreader
Propane torch
Adhesion promoter
Fiberglass cloth
Duct tape

Safety Equipment

Safety glasses
Dust respirator
Leather gloves

Procedure

Task Completed

1. To determine if a part has an olefin component, sand the backside of the part with 80 grit paper on a dual-action sander. If the part melts or smears, it contains olefin. A TPO part obviously contains olefin. ❑

2. Wash the front and back of the part with soap and water. Then clean it with a plastic cleaner. ❑

3. If the part is not damaged, cut it with a hacksaw or cut off tool Align the front side of the repair with duct tape. ❑

4. Hand sand the back side two inches on either side of the cut with 80 grit paper. ❑

5. The plastic must be treated to form a good bond with the repair material. One method is to use an aerosol adhesion promoter. This must be sprayed on each time the part is sanded. The repair material must be applied quickly. ❑

6. The other way to prepare the surface is to flame treat with a propane torch. The torch should be passed quickly over the surface to remove contaminants. Then the repair material must be applied quickly. ❑

7. Cut out two pieces of fiberglass cloth the size of the repair area. Mix the flexible repair material. Put on a coat of material. Then lay the fiberglass cloth on it. Work the cloth into the material with a body filler spreader. Apply another coat of material followed by the last piece of cloth. Again work the cloth into the material. Spread a final coat of material over the cloth. Allow to cure. ❑

8. Remove the duct tape from the front side. Sand a bevel into the cut. Sand out about one inch on either side of the cut. ❑

9. Apply adhesion promoter or flame treat. Overfill the cut with flexible repair
    material. Allow to cure.   ❑

10. Sand with 80 grit paper. Then featheredge the paint with 220 grit paper, followed
    by 400 grit paper.   ❑

Review Questions

Name_____ Date _____ Instructor Review _____

1. Plastics that sand "greasy" must have an

   _____

   to make the filler stick.

2. Thermoplastics can be welded.

   A. True
   B. False

3. The symbol TPO means _____.

4. When repairing urethane, Technician A uses
   a flexible repair material. Technician B uses
   a rigid repair material. Who is correct?

   A. Technician A
   B. Technician B
   C. Both A and B
   D. Neither A nor B

5. When repairing SMC, Technician A uses
   body filler. Technician B uses rigid repair
   material. Who is correct?

   A. Technician A
   B. Technician B
   C. Both A and B
   D. Neither A nor B

6. ABS is best repaired by welding.

   A. True
   B. False

7. PP is a thermoset plastic.

   A. True
   B. False

8. When splicing SMC, Technician A uses a
   backing strip. Technician B leaves a $1/4$" gap
   between the panels. Who is correct?

   A. Technician A
   B. Technician B
   C. Both A and B
   D. Neither A nor B

9. Technician A states that a two-sided weld is
   the strongest. Technician B believes that
   when making a two-sided weld, must
   V-groove both sides. Who is correct?

   A. Technician A
   B. Technician B
   C. Both A and B
   D. Neither A nor B

10. PUR can be repaired be welding.

    A. True
    B. False

Chapter 15

Other Body Shop Repairs

Shop Assignment 15-1

Name_____ Date _____ Instructor Review _____

Air Bags

1. List the function of the following parts:
   A. Impact sensor
   B. Safeing sensor
   C. Wiring harness
   D. Clock spring

2. The air bags have been deployed in a 1995 Ford Escort. List the components that must be replaced.

   _____

   _____

   _____

   List the components that must be checked.

   _____

   _____

   _____

3. The air bags have been deployed in a 1995 Chrysler Lebaron. List the components that must be replaced.

   _____

   _____

   _____

   List the components that must be checked.

   _____

   _____

   _____

Job Sheet 15-1

Name_____ Date _____ Instructor Review _____

Stripe Tape Installation

Objective

After completing this lab, the student should be able to install pin stripes.

Equipment

A car
Stripe tape
Wax and grease remover

Safety Equipment

Safety glasses

Procedure

Task Completed

1. Wash the car. Degrease the area where the stripes will be placed. ❑

2. Measure out the needed amount of stripe. Measure each panel with the stripe tape. Add on an extra foot in length. ❑

3. Remove the paper backing from the front six inches of the stripe tape. This exposes the sticky surface. ❑

4. Place the stripe tape at the desired location at the front of the car. ❑

5. Pull the paper backing off and lay the stripe in place. Do not push on the tape at this time. The tape must only lightly adhere to the surface at this point. ❑

6. Lay the stripe on the entire side of the vehicle. If you follow the body lines, the stripe may have an arch. The other option is to make a straight line. ❑

7. Sight down the side of the car by standing at the rear and looking with one eye. Check for any sags. Move away from the car at least ten feet and check for sags or out of level. Make any corrections. ❑

8. When you are satisfied with the fit, rub the stripe into place to lock it on. ❑

9. Remove the clear plastic film on top of the stripe. Be careful! Do not lift the stripe off of the surface. ❑

10. Cut the stripe at the door openings. Fold the stripe around the corners. ❑

Job Sheet 15-2

Name_____ Date _____ Instructor Review _____

Glued-On Molding Installation

Objective

After completing this lab, the student should be able to remove and replace wide moldings.

Equipment

Car with molding
Propane torch
Putty knife
220 grit sandpaper
Grinder
Molding tape
Wax and grease remover
Masking tape

Safety Equipment

Safety glasses

Procedure

Task Completed

1. Check the molding to see if it is bolted on. Some moldings are bolted and glued. Remove the nuts from the bolts. ❑

2. Use the propane torch to heat the putty knife. You do not need to heat it to a cherry red color, just enough to make it hot. ❑

3. Slide the putty knife in between the molding and the car. When the knife cools, reheat it. Try not to dig a corner of the knife into the paint. Remove the molding. ❑

4. Examine the molding. If it has a metal backing, the molding will be permanently bent. To correct this, use a slow speed grinder to remove the metal backing. The molding will now be pliable enough to straighten. ❑

5. Remove all of the old molding tape from the back of the molding. Any molding tape left on will result in a failure. A hot putty knife or a wax/grease remover can be used. ❑

6. Wash the car. Clean the area where the molding will be placed with a wax and grease remover. ❑

7. Lightly sand the back side of the molding with 220 grit sand paper. Stretch out the molding tape on the molding. Cover as much of the area as possible. Leave the plastic covering on the tape until the molding is ready to be installed. ❑

8. Place masking tape as a guide on the car where the bottom of the molding will be placed. Step back from the car. Check the tape for level. Make any corrections and test fit the molding. ❑

9. Remove the plastic covering on the molding tape. Some moldings are cut to allow the door to open. Make sure that you allow this possibility. Use the tape as a guide to start the molding application. ❑

10. Stretch the moldings as you apply it. Push into place, then remove the masking tape. ❑

Job Sheet 15-3

Name_____ Date _____ Instructor Review _____

Leaks

Objective

After completing this lab, the student should be able to diagnose and repair wind noise and water leaks.

Equipment

Car with a narrow window frame
Car with a water leak in the trunk
Car with a roof leak
Block of wood
Tracing powder or chalk

Safety Equipment

Safety glasses

Procedure

Task Completed

1. Road test the car to determine if there is any wind noise. To check for fit, open the door and hold a dollar bill or a piece of paper so it hangs into the upper opening. Then shut the door on the dollar bill. Pull out on it. If it pulls out with considerable drag, the door is adjusted properly. If the dollar bill tears, the door is fitted too tightly. If it slips out with little effort, the door is too loose. ❑

2. To make wind noise and water leaks in an undamaged car, open the door, roll down the window, and place a 2" x 4" block of wood at the top of the window frame opening. Close the door against the wood. Push on the door. This motion will move the window frame out and should give you a wind noise. ❑

3. Road test the car. Use the dollar bill test again. ❑

4. To correct this problem, open the door and roll down the window. Place a 2" x 4" block of wood in between the door and the center pillar. Do not place it on the window frame. Push in on the window frame. ❑

5. Road test the car and check the door with a dollar bill. Repeat the procedure until the problem is fixed. ❑

6. For a quick check of a water leak in the trunk, spread tracing powder or chalk on the trunk gasket. Shut the deck lid. Open and check the inside of the deck lid for powder. Any places where the powder is not present on the lid are potential leaks. Place a block of wood under where the gasket is mounted and tap upwards with a hammer. ❑

7. Another test for water leaks in a trunk is to have one worker inside the trunk with a flashlight. Shut the deck lid and pour water over the deck lid. The worker inside can determine the positions of the leaks. ❑

8. For leaks or noise on sunroofs or t-tops, remove the glass portion. In most leak cases, the gaskets are worn out or misshapen. Test with water. ❑

9. If the gaskets are found to be defective, unbolt and cut out the bad gasket. Glue in and rebolt new gaskets. ❑

10. Be sure to recheck with a water test. ❑

Job Sheet 15-4

Name_____ Date _____ Instructor Review _____

Gasketed Glass Removal and Installation

Objective

After completing this lab, the student should be able to remove and reinstall gasketed glass, such as the back glass on a pickup truck.

Equipment

A vehicle in need of glass replacement
Replacement glass and gasket
Soap and water
Nylon push stick

Safety Equipment

Safety glasses

Procedure

Task Completed

1. Pull on the one corner of the gasket. The gasket should pull out and the glass will follow. If it does not, use a nylon push stick to help. ❑

2. Once the glass has begun to pull out from one corner, the rest will pull out easily. ❑

3. Examine the flange. Clean as needed. Check the new glass and gasket for damage. ❑

4. Put soap and water inside the gasket. ❑

5. Slide the new gasket into one corner. ❑

6. From the inside, slide the push stick along the inside portion of the gasket. ❑

7. Work around the edge of the window. ❑

8. From the outside, push the gasket into place. ❑

9. Use the push stick to straighten the edges. ❑

10. Check for leaks with a water hose. ❑

Job Sheet 15-5

Name_____ Date _____ Instructor Review _____

Urethane Glass Full Cut-out

Objective

After completing this lab, the student should be able to remove and replace a urethane bonded windshield.

Equipment

Car in need of windshield replacement
Music wire and handles
Hook tool
Power cut-out tool

Safety Equipment

Safety glasses

Procedure

Task Completed

1. Remove the rear view mirror, windshield wipers and cowl vent panel (if it has one). ❑

2. Find the end of the windshield molding. Use a hook tool to remove one end. Carefully pull the molding out from around the entire windshield. In most cases, the molding cannot be reused. ❑

3. If you are using music wire to cut the urethane, push the insertion tool and wire to the outside. Attach the handles at either end. ❑

4. If you are using a power cut-out tool, sharpen the blade first. Use a utility knife to score the inside of the urethane. Insert the tool into the urethane from inside the car. ❑

5. With either method, cut around the entire windshield. Be watchful of broken glass. Keep the wire or cutter next to the glass. When the windshield is loose, push it out. ❑

6. Remove all of the urethane from the flange. Cut with a utility knife or tool. Check the flange for rust. If rust is present, sand it down. ❑

7. Test fit the new windshield. When the alignment is correct, stretch a piece of masking tape from the roof to the windshield and from the A pillar to the windshield. Cut the tape. These will serve as alignment marks. Remove the windshield. ❑

8. Clean the flange with a urethane adhesive cleaner. Apply a urethane primer to the flange. Clean the inside of the new windshield. Put on a urethane primer where the windshield will be bonded to the flange. ❑

9. Place a $5/16$" x $5/16$" square ribbon sealer to the inside edge of the flange. ❑

10. A fast curing, high strength urethane can now be applied around the outside of the square ribbon sealer. Cut the tube at a 45 degree angle. ❑

11. Install the windshield using the alignment marks. Press the glass to contact the square ribbon sealer and the urethane. ❑

12. Check for urethane squeezing out along the edges of the windshield. Use a paddle to wipe off any excess and to fill any voids. At least one-fourth of an inch all the way around the windshield must be bonded to the urethane. ❑

13. Replace the molding. Reinstall the cowl vent panel, the windshield wipers, and the rear view mirror. ❑

Job Sheet 15-6

Name_____ Date _____ Instructor Review _____

Encapsulated Quarter Glass Repair

Objective

After completing this lab, the student should be able to remove and replace encapsulated glass.

Equipment

Car with quarter glass
$5/_{16}$" x $5/_{16}$" square ribbon sealer
Utility knife
Paddle
Cut out tool
Urethane
Duct tape

Safety Equipment

Safety glasses

Procedure

Task Completed

1. Remove the interior trim for access to the quarter window. Some vehicles may require extensive disassembly. ❑

2. Examine the inside of the window. It may be bolted in place. If nuts are present, remove them. Remove the screws that may be holding the molding also. The cutting will be done from the inside. Place duct tape on the outside to hold the window in place. ❑

3. Select a blade size that will cut through the urethane only and not reach the plastic molding. Sharpen the blade of the cut out tool. ❑

4. Score the urethane next to the window using a utility knife. ❑

5. Insert the blade in the urethane and begin cutting. ❑

6. Work around the window. Be careful not to cut through the molding. If the molding is glued on, cut behind the molding. When the window is loose, go outside of the car and remove the duct tape and the window. ❑

7. Remove the urethane on the flange with a utility knife. Clean with a urethane cleaner. Prime with a urethane primer. Clean the inside of the window and the prime area to be bonded with a urethane primer. ❑

8. Install $5/16$" x $5/16$" square ribbon sealer to the inside edge of the opening. Apply a one-fourth inch bead of fast, curing high strength urethane to the outside of the sealer. If the molding was bonded, apply a bead of urethane to its mating surface. ❑

9. Press the window into place. Use a paddle to fill any voids in the urethane. Remove any excess. ❑

10. Reinstall the nuts or screws. Replace the interior. ❑

Review Questions

Name_____ Date _____ Instructor Review _____

1. Exterior windshield moldings are also called _____ _____ .

2. When replacing an adhesive bonded windshield, Technician A uses the partial cut out method. Technician B uses the full cut out method. Who is correct?

   A. Technician A
   B. Technician B
   C. Both A and B
   D. Neither A nor B

3. _____ glass is used for windshields.

4. Technician A cleans old adhesive from a windshield with denatured alcohol. Technician B believes extensive rust in the pinch weld area will require the full cut out method. Who is correct?

   A. Technician A
   B. Technician B
   C. Both A and B
   D. Neither A nor B

5. Technician A replaces a riveted-in window with bolts. Technician B believes only rivets may be used to replace rivets. Who is correct?

   A. Technician A
   B. Technician B
   C. Both A and B
   D. Neither A nor B

6. Technician A states water leaks are usually caused by a damaged weather strip. Technician B believes a door that shuts too tightly can cause a water leak. Who is correct?

   A. Technician A
   B. Technician B
   C. Both A and B
   D. Neither A nor B

7. A _____ is attached to the vehicle frame with energy absorbing bolts and brackets.

8. A retractor can be tested by driving the car at a slow speed and rapidly stopping.

   A. True
   B. False

9. The _____ produces a small spark when an electrical signal is sent from a control unit.

10. Undamaged air bag sensors do not need to be replaced.

    A. True
    B. False

Chapter 16

Restoring Corrosion Protection

Job Sheet 16-1

Name_____ Date _____ Instructor Review _____

Surface Rust Removal

Objective

After completing this lab, the student should be able to recognize and repair rust damage.

Equipment

Rusted vehicle
80, 220, 320, 400, 600 grit paper
Grinder
Scratch awl
Polyester glazing
Rubber gloves
Metal prep
Sand blaster
Coarse scratch pad
Urethane primer
Spray gun
Self etch primer
Hard block
Sealer
Spot putty
Razor blade

Safety Equipment

Safety glasses
Dust respirator
Leather gloves

Procedure

Task Completed

1. Wash the car. Examine the vehicle for rust. Rust usually begins in the door hem flanges where the body panels meet or under the moldings. Occasionally, it may be found in the center of a panel due to paint damage. Bubbles in the paint indicate rust.   ❏

2. Probe the bubbles with a scratch awl. There will be dark colored steel in them. This is the rust. Many times the metal will be so weak, the awl will pierce the metal. In that case, cut out the metal and weld in a new panel. If the awl does not pierce the metal, you have found surface rust. Use the grinder to remove the paint from the area. Sometimes the rust arms extend outward from a central location. Make sure you find all traces of rust. Featheredge the paint edge with 80, 220, and 400 grit paper.   ❏

3. Sand blast all of the rust. There will be numerous pits in the metal. Sand blast until the dark color has been removed from the rust.   ❏

4. Mix the metal etch according to directions on the bottle. Normally the ration is one part etch to two parts water. Load this mixture into a spray bottle. Wear rubber gloves as you spray the sand blasted area with etch solution. Work the surface with a coarse scratch pad. Keep the surface wet for five minutes. Wipe off the area.   ❏

5. Mask off the area. Mix the self etching primer, according to the directions on the can. Usually it is one part primer to one part converter. Load this mixture into a spray gun. Spray two wet coats on the bare metal. Allow proper flash time between coats.   ❏

6. Mix up a urethane primer according to the directions on the can. Load this mixture into the spray gun and apply three coats, allowing the proper flash time. Spray on a guide coat. Allow an appropriate cure time.   ❏

7. Sand the guide coat with 320 dry paper on a hard block. If pits are visible in the primer after sanding, use a polyester glazing putty to fill them.   ❏

8. Mix the putty according to the directions on the can. It is usually mixed like body filler. Use a razor blade to apply the putty, instead of a body filler spreader. The razor blade is better at filling the small pits. Avoid any excess. Excess putty requires more sanding. Allow adequate cure time.   ❏

9. Sand the glazing putty with 320 grit paper on a hard block. Cross cut this area with 600 grit paper.   ❏

10. Spray a coat of sealer over the primed area. The surface is ready for a top coat.   ❏

Job Sheet 16-2

Name_____ Date _____ Instructor Review _____

Corrosion Prevention Enclosed Rail

Objective

After completing this lab, the student should be able to properly treat a spliced rail for prevention of corrosion.

Equipment

Spliced fame rail
Epoxy primer
220 grit paper
Rust proofing wax
Rust proof spray wand
Blow gun
Abrasive pad

Safety Equipment

Safety glasses
Paint respirator
Impervious gloves
Paint suit

Procedure

Task Completed

1. This exercise will cover a spliced joint that is not accessible. Accessible joints—those visible at the front of the rail—are treated in the same manner. ❑

2. Remove the weld scale from the joint by directing the air from a blow gun into the rail. You may also use a long-handled brush to reach into the rail to remove the heat blistered paint. The purpose is to expose the bare metal for treatment. ❑

3. Clean the outside of the rail at the weld joint with an abrasive pad. Remove all of the blistered paint. Feather the paint edge with 220 grit paper. ❑

4. Mix the epoxy primer according to the directions on the can. Usually this is one part primer to one part converter. Load this mixture into the wand canister. Insert the wand into the rail. Make sure the wand is inserted beyond the joint. Pull the trigger to start the spray. Pull the wand toward you. Release the trigger before you reach the end of the rail. ❑

5. Spray the outside of the rail with the epoxy primer in a conventional spray gun. Allow the proper flash time. ❑

6. Mix the top coat according to specifications. Load this mixture into the wand canister. Spray the top coat in the same manner as the primer. ❑

7. Spray the outside of the rail with a top coat in a conventional spray gun. Allow the paint to dry overnight. ❑

8. Load the wand canister with rust proofing wax. Spray inside the rail as before. ❑

Review Questions

Name_____ Date _____ Instructor Review _____

1. Rust on a unibody car can affect the safety of the passengers.

   A. True
   B. False

2. Chemical corrosion requires three elements:

   _____,

   _____, and

   _____.

3. Technician A states that galvanizing protects steel from rust. Technician B believes if galvanized steel is scratched, it can rust. Who is correct?

   A. Technician A
   B. Technician B
   C. Both A and B
   D. Neither A nor B

4. Technician A states that galvanized coating is lost during welding. Technician B believes galvanized coating is lost during grinding. Who is correct?

   A. Technician A
   B. Technician B
   C. Both A and B
   D. Neither A nor B

5. Corrosion happens faster at lower temperatures.

   A. True
   B. False

6. Technician A applies undercoating to bare metal. Technician B sprays bare metal with self-etching primer. Then he sprays it with undercoating. Who is correct?

   A. Technician A
   B. Technician B
   C. Both A and B
   D. Neither A nor B

7. Technician A sprays two wet coats of self-etching primer. Technician B sprays a tack coat followed by a medium wet coat. Who is correct?

   A. Technician A
   B. Technician B
   C. Both A and B
   D. Neither A nor B

8. Which of these primers gives a better protection against corrosion?

   A. Self-etching primer
   B. Epoxy primer

9. Technician A sprays the inside of the frame rails with self-etching primer. Technician B uses epoxy primer. Who is correct?

   A. Technician A
   B. Technician B
   C. Both A and B
   D. Neither A nor B

10. Acid rain means the rain water has a high PH.

   A. True
   B. False

Chapter 17

Vehicle Surface Preparation

Job Sheet 17-1

Name_____ Date _____ Instructor Review _____

Masking

Objective

After completing this lab, the student should be able to mask a vehicle for repainting.

Equipment

Four-door car
Paper machine 3", 18" paper
2" masking tape
Tire covers
Fine line paper
Liquid mask

Safety Equipment

Safety glasses

Procedure

Task Completed

1. Sprayed paint will find its way onto every surface you do not protect. A good masking job will not only protect the vehicle, but also will not have any folds or crevices that may trap dirt. ❏

2. This exercise will mask off the side of a four-door car to simulate a repaint of the entire side including the rocker panel. Wash the car and flow it off. ❏

3. Begin masking by opening the doors, hood and deck lid. Start the ³/₄" tape at the front of the rocker panel. Apply a continuous strip all the way to the dog leg. Roll the outside edge of the tape back. This is called "back taping" It will allow a soft paint edge. Place 3" paper on the tape to keep the paint off of the rocker panel inside the door. ❏

4. Mask off the center pillar by wrapping the paper around the upper portion. Use 3" paper to mask the rear inner edge of both doors. On the rear door, also mask the front inner edge. Do not allow the tape to wrap around the door edge. ❏

5. Apply the 3" paper to the inner edge of the windshield pillar, the inner edge of the roof drip rail and the inner edge of the sail panel. Also mask off the inner edges of both window frames. The tape sticks to metal easier than it sticks to rubber. Wiping the weatherstrip with thinner usually helps with the tape adhesion.   ❏

6. Close the doors and make sure all of the paper stays inside the doors. Mask the windows by outlining the weather strip with tape. Use 18" paper. Start in the rear of the front window. Apply the paper all of the way to the front lower corner. Neatly fold or cut the paper to fit. Then tape off the loose edges at the rear and at the bottom. Be sure to tape over any of the paper folds to keep the dirt out. Tape the rear window in the same manner.   ❏

7. Apply 3" paper to the under hood fender flange. Use 2" tape on the hood flange. Close the hood. Tape 18" paper down the entire hood edge. Mask the windshield at the edge. Then mask the grille and bumper. Remember to neatly fold and tape to keep the dirt out.   ❏

8. Mask the inner channel in the deck lid with 3" paper. For the next step, mask the tail lights and rear bumper. Close the lid. Apply 18" paper to the entire deck lid side and the edge of the rear window.   ❏

9. Mask the roof at the edge in the same manner as the hood and the deck lid. Liquid mask or plastic sheet can be applied to the remainder of the hood, roof and deck lid.   ❏

10. Mask the door handles and locks by wrapping them with tape. Marker lights can be masked, cutting the tape to fit. Wheel houses can be sprayed with liquid mask. Tire covers should be placed over the tires.   ❏

Job Sheet 17-2

Name_____ Date _____ Instructor Review _____

Surface Prep Scratch

Objective

After completing this lab, the student should be able to properly repair a scratch.

Equipment

Fender
Guide coat
Spray gun
Urethane primer
80, 220, 400, 600 grit paper
Sanding block
Wax/grease remover
Self etch primer
DA
Nail
Respirator

Safety Equipment

Safety glasses
Dust respirator
Leather gloves
Supplied air respirator
Impervious gloves
Paint suit

Procedure

Task Completed

1. Obtain a fender. Use a nail to put a 12" scratch in the panel. The scratch must be etched into the metal.   ❏

2. Clean the fender with soap and water. Dry off. Then use a wax and grease remover. Apply with a spray bottle and wipe off before the panel dries.   ❏

3. Featheredge the scratch with 80 grit paper on a jitterbug or finish dual-action sander. Sand out about two inches from the scratch. Be sure to keep the sander flat. Do not dig into the paint.   ❏

4. Sand over the 80 grit scratches with 180 or 220 grit paper. Work out from the scratch. Continue sanding about ¹/₂" beyond where the 80 grit scratches with 180 or 220 grit paper. Work out from the scratch. Continue sanding about ¹/₂" beyond where the 80 grit paper stopped.   ❏

5. Final sand with 320 or 400 grit paper. Sand out from the scratch to about ¹/₂" beyond where the 220 grit paper stopped. There should be at least 1" of each pain layer showing. This is to make sure that there is a gradual change in height.   ❏

6. Clean off the sanding dust and spray two coats of self-etching primer over the bare metal.   ❏

7. When the self-etching primer has flashed off, spray a urethane primer. Use one coat of urethane for each paint layer.   ❏

8. Dust a contrasting color over the primer to serve as a guide coat.   ❑

9. Block sand the urthane primer with 320 grit paper on a hard block.   ❑

10. Finish sanding the urethane primer with 600 grit paper and water. Remove all 320
    grit scratches.   ❑

Job Sheet 17-3

Name_____ Date _____ Instructor Review _____

Paint Urethane Replacement Bumper

Objective

After completing this lab, the student should be able to properly refinish a urethane replacement bumper.

Equipment

Replacement urethane bumper
Wax and grease remover
Rubbing alcohol and water
Coarse scratch pad
Sealer
Base coat
Clear coat
Spray gun
Tack rag

Safety Equipment

Safety glasses
Supplied air respirator
Impervious gloves
Paint suit

Procedure

Task Completed

1. Examine the replacement urethane bumper for damage. Then clean with a wax and grease remover. ❑

2. Mix one part rubbing alcohol with one part water. This solution will remove the mold release compound. Wipe off the bumper with the alcohol/water solution. ❑

3. Wet sand the bumper with a coarse scratch pad or 400 grit sand paper. Use the alcohol/water solution for the wet sanding. Make sure that all areas are sanded. ❑

4. Clean off the sanding sludge with a wax and grease remover or water. Mount the bumper on a saw horse. Blow it off and then tack it off. ❑

5. Spray a sealer on the bumper. Check for the recommended type of sealer. It is important to seal the bumper within thirty minutes of the final sanding. After thirty minutes, additional mold release compound could be present. ❑

6. After the sealer has dried, nib sand off any dirt or dry spots. Tack. ❑

7. Check to see if a flex agent is required in the base coat. Usually flex agent is not needed. Spray the base coat. At least three coats are needed. Allow proper flash time between coats. ❑

8. Check to see if flex agent is required in the clear coat. Mix the flex agent with the clear and hardener. ❑

9. Tack off the dried base coat. Spray two coats of flexed clear. ❑

Job Sheet 17-4

Name_____ Date _____ Instructor Review _____

Trimming Parts

Objective

After completing this lab, the student should be able to trim in parts prior to installation on a vehicle.

Equipment

New fender hood, door or deck lid
Sealer
Base coat
Clear coat
Respirator
Scratch pad
Paint gun
Wax/grease remover

Safety Equipment

Safety glasses
Paint respirator
Impervious gloves
Paint suit

Procedure

Task Completed

1. Check the new part for dents. Make sure it is the correct part. ❑

2. Check the original part to see what areas are painted. You must put color on the new part to match what is painted on the original part. ❑

3. Clean the part with a wax and grease remover. ❑

4. Sand all areas of the part that will be painted with a coarse scratch pad or 400 grit paper. Remove all shiny spots and then remove all sanding residue. ❑

5. Mount the part on a saw horse. Blow the part off and tack. ❑

6. Spray on a sealer or epoxy primer over the entire sanded area. Consult your paint systems manual for the recommended material. ❑

7. Spray base coat on the areas that cannot be sprayed after the part is mounted on the car. On a fender, this would be the flange under the hood and the lip visible when the door is opened. You should also spray the front flange, the wheel well lip and the bottom areas. On a door, spray the window channel and inner surfaces. On a hood or deck lid, spray the inside and edge flange. Allow proper flash between coats. ❑

8. Some paint manufacturers make a single part edging clear. It is meant to be sprayed on areas that will not be in the sunlight. Simply load it into the gun and spray it on. ❑

9. Spray clear coat over the base coat. Avoid getting clear coat on the primer. If clear coat is on the primer, it will have to be sanded off. ❑

Review Questions

Name_____ Date _____ Instructor Review _____

1. The paint job is only as good as the primer beneath it.

   A. True
   B. False

2. Technician A states that silicon carbide sandpaper should be used to sand metal. Technician B believes aluminum oxide sandpaper is better to sand metal. Who is correct?

   A. Technician A
   B. Technician B
   C. Both A and B
   D. Neither A nor B

3. Open coat sandpaper is used for wet sanding.

   A. True
   B. False

4. Technician A uses a 24 grit disk to grind rust. Technician B uses a 80 grit disk on a dual-action sander to sand body filler. Who is correct?

   A. Technician A
   B. Technician B
   C. Both A and B
   D. Neither A nor B

5. Wet sanding cuts paint faster than dry sanding.

   A. True
   B. False

6. A _____ is a light coat of contrasting color intended to show defects.

7. A "Bullseye" results from improper feather-edging.

   A. True
   B. False

8. Technician A uses a spray bottle to apply a wax and grease remover. Technician B uses a rag to apply a wax and grease remover. Who is correct?

   A. Technician A
   B. Technician B
   C. Both A and B
   D. Neither A nor B

9. Technician A wears gloves when rubbing bare metal. Technician B believes that cleaning the bare metal with a wax and grease remover will eliminate oil from the hands. Who is correct?

   A. Technician A
   B. Technician B
   C. Both A and B
   D. Neither A nor B

10. Pot life decreases as temperature increases.

    A. True
    B. False

Chapter 18

Refinishing Equipment and Its Use

Shop Assignment 18-1

Name_____ Date _____ Instructor Review _____

Paint Gun Parts

1.

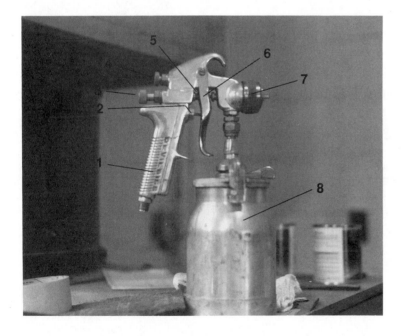

Name these parts

1._____

2._____

3._____

4._____

5._____

6._____

7._____

8._____

2.

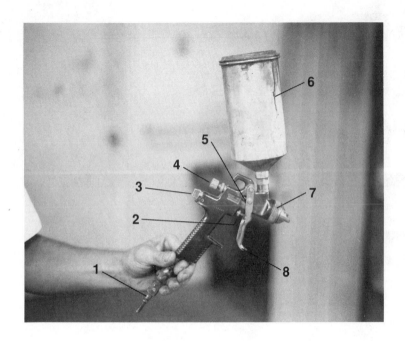

1. _____

2. _____

3. _____

4. _____

5. _____

6. _____

7. _____

8. _____

3. Explain external mix. _____

_____

_____

_____

4. Your instructor will demonstrate how to properly clean a paint gun. Summarize the procedure in a paragraph. _____

_____

_____

_____

_____

_____

Job Sheet 18-1

Name_____ Date _____ Instructor Review _____

Water Guns

Objective

After completing this lab, the student should be able to adjust and use a spray gun.

Equipment

Spray gun
Fender
Hood
Video camera

Safety Equipment

Safety glasses

Procedure

Task Completed

1. Place a fender on a saw horse so that it hangs vertically. ❑

2. Fill a paint gun with water. Adjust the gun as follows: ❑

   A. Set fan size. If the area to be painted is small, turn the fan adjustment—screw in. If the area to be painted is large, such as a complete paint job, turn the screw out.

   B. Set air pressure. The paint manufacturer's manual will list the proper air pressure. Set your gun at the required air pressure. For the water gun, set the air at 40 p.s.i. at the gun.

   C. Material control. Set the material control knob to fill the fan with water. Adjust the knob in and out and watch how the amount of material changes.

3. When the gun is set up, hold the paint gun in one hand and the air hose in the other hand. This is to keep the hose out of the way. Position yourself off center as you face the fender. You will pivot with your legs rather than relying totally on your arm movements. This will give the paint job a more uniform finish as well as prevent fatigue. ❑

4. Keep the gun a hands-width away from the panel. Practice maintaining this uniform distance. ❑

5. Position the gun off the edge of the fender. Begin spraying by pulling the trigger. Move across the panel. Overlap each coat by fifty percent. ❑

6. The fan must hit the panel evenly. If the gun is tilted, the spray is dry at one end of the fan and wet at the other end. This is called "heeling" in your textbook. If you stand in one place and just pivot your arm, you will again be too wet in one area and dry in another. This is called "arcing" in your textbook. ❑

7. You will need to adjust the gun angle as you spray to make sure the fan hits the surface uniformly. ❑

8. Set up a hood on two saw horses. Practice on the hood. To prevent "heeling", you must bend your wrist. It will seem awkward at first, but it will give better spray results. Start at one side of the hood, spray to the center. Then move to the other side and spray from the center to the edge.   ❑

9. Have a lab partner observe your spray technique. Make the necessary adjustments.   ❑

10. The instructor may video tape each of the students spraying, so they can observe their own techniques.   ❑

Job Sheet 18-2

Name_____ Date _____ Instructor Review _____

Paint Spray Technique

Objective

After completing this lab, the student should be able to properly operate a spray gun.

Equipment	Safety Equipment
Fender	Safety glasses
Hood	Paint respirator
Wax/Grease remover	Impervious gloves
400 grit paper	Paint suit
Spray gun	
Enamel paint, solid and metallic	
Reducer	

Procedure

Task Completed

1. Obtain a fender and hood. Clean and then sand both panels with 400 grit paper. Reclean and place the panels on a saw horse. ❏

2. Mix a single stage, solid color enamel according to directions on the can. Load the paint gun. Put on your paint safety equipment. ❏

3. Set up the gun in the same manner as the water gun. Set the fan, air pressure and then the material. ❏

4. Proper spray technique is a balance of gun adjustment, movement, and distance. If you move too fast or are too far away, then the paint will go on dry. If you move too slow or are too close, then the paint will run. ❏

5. Position yourself in front of the fender so that you can comfortably reach the entire area. Hold the gun a hand's width away from the panel. Trigger the gun and move across the panel. Trigger off when you move off of the panel. Look carefully at the surface. If it is rough and dry, then you moved too quickly or were too far away. If you had runs, then you moved too slowly or were too close. A little "orange peel" is acceptable in enamel. ❏

6. Adjust your spray technique in order to put on a uniform, smooth finish with a minimum or "orange peel." ❏

7. Spray the hood noting that it is more difficult to get a run in it. It is also harder to get the paint to flow out. ❏

8. When you have mastered solid color, you can spray a metallic enamel. Mix up a light metallic color such as silver. Load the paint into the gun. ❏

9. Spray the fender with the metallic paint. You may notice that the aluminum flakes will sag and leave a discoloration or dark spot. This can be eliminated with an additional coat of paint.   ❏

10. Spray the hood, Streaks of light and dark are called "tiger stripes." These can be eliminated by spraying successive coats at an angle. This tends to cover up and blend in the stripes. Another method is to turn the paint gun material control knob in. This makes the gun spray drier. A different method is to mist coat by holding the gun further away from the panel. This also helps in setting the metallic.   ❏

Review Questions

Name_____ Date _____ Instructor Review _____

1. The second stage of atomization occurs when the paint stream is struck by jets of air from the air cap horns.

   A. True
   B. False

2. The _____
   adjusts the fan size.

3. Technician A uses a gravity feed gun for primer. Technician B uses a siphon for primer. Who is correct?

   A. Technician A
   B. Technician B
   C. Both A and B
   D. Neither A nor B

4. If the air valve sticks, the trigger will no longer control the air flow.

   A. True
   B. False

5. If a siphon feed gun does not spray properly, the first item you should check is the cup vent hole.

   A. True
   B. False

6. It is easier to spray upside down with a pressure pot system.

   A. True
   B. False

7. Viscosity is measured with a Chevy cup.

   A. True
   B. False

8. The proper way to adjust a paint gun is to set the fan, followed by _____.
   Then _____.

9. _____ means the painter is not holding the gun perpendicular to the surface.

10. Technician A states solvent pop is a common problem with HVLP guns. Technician B believes HVLP paint guns save on material. Who is correct?

    A. Technician A
    B. Technician B
    C. Both A and B
    D. Neither A nor B

Chapter 19

Refinishing Procedures

Shop Assignment 19-1

Name_____ Date _____ Instructor Review _____

Paint Mixing

1.

DUPONT CHROMABASE®

CONTAINS: butyl acetate, 123-86-4; acetone, 67-64-1; methyl ethyl ketone, 78-93-3; toluene, 108-88-3; isopropyl alcohol, 67-63-0; ethyl acetate, 141-78-6; propylene glycol monomethyl ether acetate, 108-65-6; xylene, 1330-20-7; ethylene-vinyl acetate resin; cellulosic resin; acrylic polymer.
(For further information refer to Material Safety Data Sheet)

IMPORTANT: May be mixed with other components. Mixture will have hazards of both components. Before opening the packages, read all warning labels. Follow all precautions.

ATTENTION: Contains material which can cause cancer.

NOTICE: Repeated and prolonged overexposure to solvents may lead to permanent brain and nervous system damage. Eye watering, headaches, nausea, dizziness and loss of coordination are signs that solvent levels are too high. Intentional misuse by deliberately concentrating and inhaling the contents may be harmful or fatal.

Do not breathe vapor or spray mist. Do not get in eyes or on skin.

WEAR A PROPERLY FITTED VAPOR/PARTICULATE RESPIRATOR NIOSH/MSHA for use with paints (TC-23C), eye protection, gloves and protective clothing during application and until all vapor and spray mist are exhausted. In confined spaces, or in situations where continuous spray operations are typical, or if proper respirator fit is not possible, wear a positive-pressure, supplied-air respirator (NIOSH/MSHA TC-19C). In all cases, follow respirator manufacturers's directions for respirator use. Do not permit anyone without protection in the painting area.

Keep away from heat, sparks and flame. VAPOR MAY IGNITE EXPLOSIVELY. Vapor may spread long distances. Prevent build-up of vapor. Extinguish all pilot lights and turn off heaters, non-explosion proof electrical equipment and other sources of ignition during and after use and until all vapor is gone. Do not transfer contents to bottles or other unlabeled containers. Close container after each use. Use only with adequate ventilation.

FIRST AID: If affected by inhalation of vapor or spray mist, remove to fresh air. In case of eye contact, flush immediately with plenty of water for at least 15 minutes and call a physician; for skin, wash thoroughly with soap and water. If swallowed, CALL A PHYSICIAN IMMEDIATELY. DO NOT induce vomiting.

SPILL/WASTE: Absorb spill and dispose of waste or excess material according to Federal, State and local regulations.

KEEP OUT OF REACH OF CHILDREN   PHOTOCHEMICALLY REACTIVE

DIRECTIONS FOR USE

1 Part Color   +   1 Part Basemaker®   ⟶   Spray at 45 psi.

MIXING: To each quart of base color, add one quart of the appropriate Basemaker: 7160S Low Temp, 7175S Mid Temp, 7185S High Temp or 7195S Very High Temp.

PREPARATION Prepare all surfaces to be repaired using a DuPont undercoat system following recommended procedures. Finish by sanding with 400 grit paper (wet or dry).

SPOT REPAIR/BLENDING: Midcoat entire area to be repaired with one coat of 222S Mid-Coat Adhesion Promoter. Apply base color at 45 psi in 2-3 medium coats to achieve visual hiding. Extend each coat of base color beyond the previous one to achieve a tapered edge keeping within the midcoated area.

PANEL/OVERALL APPLICATION: To insure uniformity, apply 1 coat of Prime 'N Seal™ or VELVASEAL™ per label directions over entire area to be repaired. Apply base color to hiding.

Flash Basecoat 15-30 minutes before clearcoating.

TWO TONING: Flash first base color 30 minutes and then tape. Apply second color, remove tape and flash 30 minutes prior to clearcoating.

FOR VOC REGULATED AREAS: These directions refer to the use of products which may be restricted or require special mixing instructions in VOC regulated areas. Follow mixing and usage recommendations in the VOC Compliant Products Chart for your area.

(See Individual Label Directions For Use Of The Other DuPont Products)

Made in U.S.A   E-R1301   H-07017   3RF-548ABAK-040-0294

E. I. DU PONT DE NEMOURS & CO.(INC.), Wilmington, Delaware 19898
For medical & environmental information: (800) 441-7515

1. What is the spray viscosity? _____

2. At what air pressure is this material sprayed? _____

3. What safety equipment must be worn when spraying? _____

4. What basemaker is used if the shop temperature is 70 degrees? _____

5. What is the mixing ratio? _____

6. What is the pot life? _____

7. How many coats should be applied? _____

2.

DUPONT 7600 S   CHROMACLEAR® SUPER PRODUCTIVE

CONTAINS: acrylic polymer; butyl acetate, 123-86-4; methyl ethyl ketone, 78-93-3; methyl isobutyl ketone, 108-10-1; toluene, 108-88-3; xylene, 1330-20-7. When mixed with activator, also contains aliphatic polyisocyanate resin and hexamethylene diisocyanate monomer; 28182-81-2.
(For further information refer to Material Safety Data Sheet)
IMPORTANT: Must be mixed with other components. Mixture will have hazards of both components. Before opening the packages, read all warning labels. Follow all precautions.
NOTICE: Repeated and prolong overexposure to solvents may lead to permanent brain and nervous system damage. Eye watering, headaches, nausea, dizziness and loss of coordination are signs that the solvent levels are too high. Intentional misuse by deliberately concentrating and inhaling the contents may be harmful or fatal.
Do not breathe vapor or spray mist. Do not get in eyes or on skin.
WEAR A POSITIVE-PRESSURE, SUPPLIED-AIR RESPIRATOR (NIOSH/MSHA TC-19C), EYE PROTECTION, GLOVES AND PROTECTIVE CLOTHING WHILE MIXING ACTIVATOR WITH ENAMEL, DURING APPLICATION AND UNTIL ALL VAPOR AND SPRAY MIST ARE EXHAUSTED. Follow respirator manufacturer's directions for respirator use.
INDIVIDUALS WITH HISTORY OF LUNG OR BREATHING PROBLEMS OR PRIOR REACTION TO ISOCYANATES SHOULD NOT USE OR BE EXPOSED TO THIS PRODUCT. Do not permit anyone without protection in the painting area.
Keep away from heat, sparks and flame. VAPOR MAY CAUSE FLASH FIRE. Do not transfer contents to bottles or other unlabeled containers. Close container after each use. Use only with adequate ventilation.
FIRST AID: If affected by inhalation of vapor or spray mist, remove to fresh air. If breathing difficulty persists, or occurs later, consult a physician. In case of eye contact, flush immediately with plenty of water for at least 15 minutes and call a physician; for skin, wash thoroughly with soap and water. If swallowed, call a physician immediately and have label information available. DO NOT induce vomiting.
SPILL/WASTE: Absorb spill and dispose of waste or excess material according to Federal, State and local regulations.
KEEP OUT OF REACH OF CHILDREN   PHOTOCHEMICALLY REACTIVE

DIRECTIONS FOR USE
ACTIVATON: The activation ratio for 7600 S is 4 to 1. That is, to one quart of 7600 S, add ½ pint (two-4 oz. overcaps) of the appropriate activator-reducer: 7655 S Spot Activator-Reducer; 7675 S Panel Activator-Reducer; or 7695 S Multi Panel Activator-Reducer. Pot life of the activated clear is 3 hours.
APPLICATION: Stir thoroughly and strain. For spot and panel repairs, use 25-35 lbs. air pressure at the gun. For overalls, use 45-55 lbs. air pressure at the gun. Apply 2-3 medium coats. Allow 1 to 5 minutes flash between coats, depending on air flow and temperature.
FORCE DRY: Allow final coat to flash between 5-10 minutes at ambient temperatures before force drying. Force dry at 140°F (60°C) for 30 minutes. Can be polished and delivered after 2 hour cool-down.
EXPRESS DRY: Allow final coat of clear to flash 3-8 minutes at ambient temperatures. Express Dry at 120°F for 15 minutes. Can be polished and delivered after a 4 hour cool-down.
AIR DRY: Can be polished and delivered within 4-6 hours depending on ambient temperatures.
POLISHING: For dirt removal, lightly nib sand with 1500 grit paper and polish with either DuPont 600 S or 1500 S.
FISH EYES: Use up to 1 oz. of 259 S Additive per gallon of 7600 S. DO NOT USE FEE.
CLEAN UP: Clean all equipment immediately after use with DuPont lacquer thinner.
FOR VOC REGULATED AREAS: These directions refer to the use of products which may be restricted or require special mixing instructions in VOC regulated areas. Follow mixing and usage recommendations in the VOC Compliant Products Chart for your area.

Made in U.S.A.   (SEE INDIVIDUAL LABEL DIRECTIONS FOR USE OF THE OTHER DU PONT PRODUCTS)   3RF-266BBES-040-0193
F. I. DU PONT DE NEMOURS & CO. (INC.), Wilmington, Delaware 19898
For medical & environmental information: (800) 441-7515

1. What is the spray viscosity? _____

2. At what air pressure is this material sprayed? _____

3. What safety equipment must be worn when spraying? _____

4. What hardener is used if the shop temperature is 80 degrees? _____

5. What is the mixing ratio? _____

6. What is the pot life? _____

7. How many coats should be applied? _____

3.

 URO® 1140 S GRAY PRIMER FILLER

CONTAINS: titanium dioxide, 13463-67-7; zinc phosphate, 7779-90-0; magnesium silicate, 14807-96-6; barium sulfate, 7727-43-7; acrylic polymer; propylene glycol monomethyl ether acetate, 108-65-1; ethylene glycol monobutyl ether acetate, 112-07-02; xylene, 1330-20-7.

(For further information refer to Material Safety Data Sheet)

ATTENTION: Overexposure may cause blood disorders based on animal data.

IMPORTANT: Must be mixed with 1125 S Activator. Mixture will have hazards of both components. Before opening the packages, read all warning labels. Follow all precaution.

NOTICE: Repeated and prolonged exposure to solvents may lead to permanent brain and nervous system damage. Eye watering, headaches, nausea, dizziness and loss of coordination are signs that solvent levels are too high. Intentional misuse by deliberately concentrating and inhaling the contents may be harmful or fatal.

Do not breathe vapor or spray mist. Do not get in eyes or on skin.

WEAR A POSITIVE-PRESSURE, SUPPLIED-AIR RESPIRATOR (NIOSH/MSHA TC-19C), EYE PROTECTION, GLOVES AND PROTECTIVE CLOTHING WHILE MIXING ACTIVATOR WITH PRODUCT, DURING APPLICATION AND UNTIL ALL VAPOR AND SPRAY MIST ARE EXHAUSTED. Follow respirator manufacturer's directions for respirator use.

INDIVIDUALS WITH HISTORY OF LUNG OR BREATHING PROBLEMS OR PRIOR REACTION TO ISOCYANATES SHOULD NOT USE OR BE EXPOSED TO THIS PRODUCT. Do not permit anyone without protection in the painting area.

Keep away from heat, sparks and flame. VAPOR MAY CAUSE FLASH FIRE. Close container after each use. Do not transfer contents to bottles or other unlabeled containers.

FIRST AID: If affected by inhalation of vapor or spray mist, remove to fresh air. In case of eye contact, flush immediately with plenty of water for at least 15 minutes and call a physician; for skin, wash thoroughly with soap and water. If swallowed, CALL A PHYSICIAN IMMEDIATELY. DO NOT induce vomiting.

IN CASE OF: FIRE — Use water spray, foam, dry chemical or CO₂. SPILL/WASTE — Absorb spill and dispose of waste or excess material according to Federal, State and local regulations.

KEEP OUT OF REACH OF CHILDREN

PHOTOCHEMICALLY REACTIVE

DIRECTIONS FOR USE

SURFACE PREPARATION
- Clean all surfaces with water and a mild detergent.
- For substrates other than plastic or fiberglass, clean with 3900 S FIRST KLEAN™ 3919 S PRE-SOL®, or 3949 S KWIK CLEAN™ to remove wax and other contaminants. For plastic or fiberglass, clean with 2319S.
- Feather out damaged area with 180 grit D/A followed by 240 grit D/A.
- Remove sanding dust with 3901 S FINAL KLEAN™, 3939 S Lacquer & Enamel Cleaner or 3949 S KWIK CLEAN.
- Treat bare steel with KWIK PREP 2445 if VARIPRIME® is not being used. Aluminum must be treated with 2255/2265.
- Apply two coats of VARIPRIME® Self-Etching Primer.

MIXING AND APPLICATION
- Stir 1140 S thoroughly to insure a uniform mixture.
- To 4 parts of 1140 S add 1 part of 1125 S Activator. Reduce further with 1 part of 1130 S Converter or 1135 S Fast Converter. Mix thoroughly. No induction period is necessary. Pot life is 2-3 hours with 1130 S or 1-1½ hours with 1135 S. Better holdout is generally obtained using 1130 S.
- Apply 3-4 medium wet to wet coats until desired build is attained. Allow 5-10 minutes flash between coats.
- Air dry at least three hours at 70°F with 1130 S or two hours with 1135 S or bake for 30 minutes at 140°F. Allow vehicle to cool before sanding.

- Wet sand 1140 S with 400-600 grit paper depending on the topcoat. Air dry, then clean sanding sludge with 3901 S FINAL KLEAN or 3949 S KWIK CLEAN. Blow seams dry and tack wipe before topcoating.

SEALER
- If desired, 1140 S may be used as a sealer. Sand the surface with 320 grit D/A or 400 grit hard. Mix product as 4 parts 1140 S to 1 part 1125 S to 3 parts 1130 S or ChromaSystem reducers (1075 S, 1085 S, 1095 S). Flash 20-30 minutes before topcoating.

TOPCOATING
- Can be topcoated with ChromaSystem™ CENTARI® or IMRON®

RECOATING
- When recoating 1140 S with more 1140 S, sanding with 320 grit is required if primer has been force dried or if it has been allowed to air dry more than 16 hours.

CLEAN-UP
- Clean spray equipment immediately after use with DuPont Lacquer Thinner. Do not leave activated material in the gun.

FOR VOC REGULATED AREAS: These directions refer to the use of products which may be restricted or require special mixing instructions in VOC regulated areas. Follow mixing and usage recommendations in the VOC Compliant Products Chart for your area.

Made in Belgium

(See Individual Label Directions For Use Of The Other DuPont Products)

2RF-025BBAS-044-1294

1. List the components that are to be mixed together. _____

_____

2. List the ratio of each part. _____

_____

3. What is the pot life of the mixed primer? _____

4. What safety equipment must be worn when mixing and spraying? _____

_____

5. At what air pressure is this primer sprayed? _____

6. What is the dry time? _____

Job Sheet 19-1

Name_____ Date _____ Instructor Review _____

Paint Mixing

Objective

After completing this lab, the student should be able to mix two and three part paints and test viscosity.

Equipment

Base coat
Reducer
Mixing cans/sticks
Paint shaker
Zahn cup
Stop watch

Safety Equipment

Safety glasses
Paint respirator
Impervious gloves
Paint suit

Procedure

Task Completed

1. Read the mixing instructions on the paint can or paint manual. Some paints are two or three parts. Decide on how much mixed material you will need.   ❏

2. Put the base coat in a paint shaker for five minutes. If there isn't any shaker available, open the can and stir. All paint and primers must be shaken or stirred before mixing.   ❏

3. Place the mixing stick into the mixing can. Find the level on the stick for the desired amount of paint. For example, if you want to end up at the level of four, follow the fours on the stick.   ❏

4. Pour the paint into the mixing can up to the first number that you have chosen on the stick.   ❏

5. Quickly shake and add the remaining components to the mixing can. Use the numbers you have chosen.   ❏

6. Read the instructions and find the specified paint viscosity. Write that number here._____   ❏

7. To test the viscosity of the mixed paint, use a Zahn cup and a stop watch. The paint must be at room temperature. Push the cup to the bottom of the mixed paint. Pull the cup out. Begin timing as soon as the cup breaks the surface. As soon as the flow breaks, stop the timing. The number of seconds is the viscosity.   ❏

8. Mixed paint may not meet specifications. Fill in this chart: ❏

Specified Viscosity (sec)	Mixed Paint Viscosity (sec)	What Do You Do?
18	19	
18	15	
18	21	

Job Sheet 19-2

Name_____ Date _____ Instructor Review _____

Spraying Base Coat/Clear Coat

Objective

After completing this lab, the student should be able to spray a fender with BC/CC paint.

Equipment

Fender
Respirator
BC/CC paint
Tack rag
600 grit paper
Final wax/grease remover
Spray gun

Safety Equipment

Safety glasses
Supplied air respirator
Impervious gloves
Paint suit

Procedure

Task Completed

1. Use the fender prepared in Job Sheet 17-2. Sand the entire fender with 600 grit paper and water. Use a squeegee to remove the water. If the paint is still shiny after sanding, it has not been sanded enough. Sand until all of the paint is dull.   ❑

2. Clean the fender with a final clean wax and grease remover. This material does not penetrate as deeply as the first cleaning solvent. Use a spray bottle to distribute. Then wipe it off before the panel dries.   ❑

3. Some paint manufacturers recommend a sealer over the primer. Check to see if a sealer is needed. If a sealer is needed, properly mix, tack the fender off and spray a coat over the primer. When the sealer has flashed off, you are ready to spray.   ❑

4. Mix the base coat according to specification. Load into the gun. Adjust the gun for fan, air pressure and material.   ❑

5. Blow off the fender and saw horse with the air gun. Then tack the fenders off.   ❑

6. Spray one coat of paint over the primer or sealer only. Allow this to flash. Wipe the edges of the sprayed area with a tack rag. This will remove dry overspray.   ❑

7. Spray a second coat. This time, cover the entire fender. After a proper flash time, spray a third coat.   ❑

8. Clean the base coat out of the gun. Mix up a clear coat and load into the gun.   ❑

9. When the base coat has dried the required amount of time, tack off. Be careful not to dig into the paint surface.   ❑

10. Spray on two coats of clear. Observe the proper flash time between coats. Check the panel for signs of the scratch repair.   ❑

Job Sheet 19-3

Name_____ Date _____ Instructor Review _____

Paint Fender and Blend

Objective

After completing this lab, the student should be able to paint and clear coat a fender and blend the hood and door. This is a typical refinish when a fender is replaced.

Equipment

Vehicle with fender replaced
Wax/grease remover
600, 1000 grit paper
Masking tape and paper
Base coat
Respirator
Clear coat
Spray gun
Tack rag

Safety Equipment

Safety glasses
Supplied air respirator
Impervious gloves
Paint suit

Procedure

Task Completed

1. Remove the moldings name plate, and other trim from the fender, hood and door. ❏

2. Wash the car and de-wax the hood, fender, and door. ❏

3. If the fender has been replaced, it is assumed that it has been trimmed in. Sand the fender sealer with 600 grit paper. ❏

4. Sand the clear coat on the door and hood with 1000 grit wet paper or 800 grit dry paper. Sand the "orange peel" out of the clear coat. Blow out water and dust from all of the crevices and gaps. Wipe off with mild wax and grease remover. ❏

5. Mask the vehicle. Blow off and tack off. ❏

6. Spray one coat of base on the fender only. Allow this to flash. Tack off the hood and the door. ❏

7. Spray the second coat. End the second coat three to four inches out on the door and hood. Allow to flash. ❏

9. Tack off the hood, fender and door. Spray on the first coat of clear over the entire refinish area. Allow to flash. ❏

10. Spray the second coat of clear over the entire area. ❏

Job Sheet 19-4

Name_____ Date _____ Instructor Review _____

Blending Sail Panel

Objective

After completing this lab, the student should be able to melt the refinish clear coat into the original clear coat. This would usually be done when a quarter panel is replaced and the paint and clear is blended into the sail panel.

Equipment

Car
Base coat
Clear coat
Masking tape/paper
Spray gun
Adhesion promoter
Rubbing compound
Wax/grease remover
Tack rag
Respirator
Blending clear

Safety Equipment

Safety glasses
Supplied air respirator
Impervious gloves
Paint suit

Procedure

Task Completed

1. Obtain a vehicle in which the quarter panel can be painted and the sail panel blended. It is easier to melt in a narrow panel. If the panel is wider than eighteen inches, this technique is quite difficult. Do not try to melt in a large area, i.e., the roof. Clean and de-wax the car. ❏

2. If the quarter panel has been replaced, block sand primer as needed. You may need to blend the deck lid, rear bumper and the door. Use the full panel blend as in Job Sheet 19-3. Sand the area to be cleared with 1000 grit wet paper or 800 grit dry paper. In the area to be melted off, use rubbing compound from the edge of the sanding to out beyond the melt area—about three to four inches. ❏

3. Check the manufacturer's recommendations for adhesion promoter. In some cases, it is required to bind the refinish paint to the original clear coat. If adhesion promoter is required, follow the directions. It has a tendency to run, so be careful. Spray it over the rubbed area. Some manuals recommend it over the entire refinish area. ❏

4. After the surfaces have been prepped, blow off all of the cracks and crevices. Use a mild wax and grease remover to clean the areas to be painted. ❏

5. Spray the first coat of base on the primer only. Allow to flash and tack the edges. ❏

6. Spray and coat out two inches from the edge of the primer. If the space is tight, you can get by with one inch. Flash and tack the edges. ❏

7. Spray the third coat one to two inches from the second coat edge. Flash and tack all of the paint.   ❏

8. Clean the spray gun. Mix clear coat. Load the gun with clear. Mix up some clear blender in a second paint gun. This is called the "two-gun method."   ❏

9. The first coat of clear should cover all of the paint and end in the rubbed area. As soon as you spray this first coat, change guns and spray the blending clear over the dry edge of the clear coat.   ❏

10. Spray the last coat of clear out about one inch from the edge of the first coat. Again, switch guns and melt in the dry clear edge with the blending clear.   ❏

Review Questions

Name_____ Date _____ Instructor Review _____

1. Technician A plans to blend all repairs. Technician B checks the color before planning to blend. Who is correct?

   A. Technician A
   B. Technician B
   C. Both technicians
   D. Neither technician

2. Technician A states that surface prep is the most important factor in a good paint job. Technician B believes that the top coat is the most important factor. Who is correct?

   A. Technician A
   B. Technician B
   C. Both A and B
   D. Neither A nor B

3. Technician A states that spot painting is the easiest type of repair. Technician B believes that panel painting is the easiest type of repair. Who is correct?

   A. Technician A
   B. Technician B
   C. Both A and B
   D. Neither A nor B

4. Mid coat primer is also called _____.

5. Primer surfaces should be as heavy coats with little flash time between coats.

   A. True
   B. False

6. Technician A states that sealer is used to provide adhesion between the paint and the substate. Technician B believes sealer provides hold out. Who is correct?

   A. Technician A
   B. Technician B
   C. Both A and B
   D. Neither A nor B

7. Lacquer paint is more curable than enamel paint.

   A. True
   B. False

8. European cars have more paint on them than Japanese or American cars.

   A. True
   B. False

9. Technician A states a slow dry reducer is used in hot weather. Technician B believes a slow dry reducer is used in cold weather. Who is correct?

   A. Technician A
   B. Technician B
   C. Both A and B
   D. Neither A nor B

10. The required paint viscosity is 18 seconds. The tested viscosity is 15 seconds. Technician A states that you need to add reducer. Technician B believes you need to add paint. Who is correct?

    A. Technician A
    B. Technician B
    C. Both A and B
    D. Neither A nor B

Chapter 20

Color Matching and Custom Painting

Job Sheet 20-1

Name_____ Date _____ Instructor Review _____

Tri-Coat Let-Down Panel

Objective

After completing this lab, the student should be able to construct a let-down panel to check the color match on a tri-coat finished vehicle.

Equipment

3' x 3' piece of sheet metal
Self etching primer
Fine line tape
Masking paper
Spray gun
Base coat
Pearl coat
Clear coat
Tack rag
400 grit paper
Cut off tool
Masking tape

Safety Equipment

Safety glasses
Supplied air respirator
Impervious gloves
Paint suit

Procedure

Task Completed

1. Cut out a 3' x 3' piece of sheet metal. Measure carefully. The sheet metal should be flat. Remove any arch by hammering. ❑

2. Clean the sheet metal with a wax and grease remover. Scuff sand with 400 grit paper. Remove the sanding sludge by blowing off and tacking off. ❑

3. Spray a coat of self etching primer to treat the bare metal. Allow the proper flash time. ❑

**Task
Completed**

4. Mix the base coat according to the directions on the can. Load this mixture into the paint gun. Tack off the sheet metal. Spray one coat of base coat over the entire panel. Allow adequate flash time.   ❏

5. Measure at the top and bottom, one foot from the left side. Stretch the fine line tape to the mark lines. Mask off the left third of the panel, from the fine line tape to the left edge with masking paper and tape.   ❏

6. Spray another coat of base over the uncovered two-thirds section of the panel. Allow the proper flash time.   ❏

7. Measure at the top and bottom, two feet from the left edge. Stretch the fine line tape to the mark lines. Now mask off the left two-thirds area of the panel.   ❏

8. Spray a coat of base over the remaining one-third area of the panel. Remove all of the masking paper. Allow the proper flash time.   ❏

9. Mix up the pearl coat. Load this mixture into the gun. Spray one coat over the entire panel. Allow the proper flash time.   ❏

10. Measure up at the left and right sides, one foot from the bottom. Stretch the fine line tape to the mark lines. Mask off the lower one-third area of the panel.   ❏

11. Spray a coat of pearl over the exposed two-thirds of the panel. Allow adequate flash time.   ❏

12. Measure up at the left and right sides, two feet from the bottom of the panel. Stretch fine line tape to the mark lines. Mask off the lower two-thirds area of the panel.   ❏

13. Spray a coat of pearl over the remaining one-third area of the panel. Remove all of the masking paper. Allow the proper flash time.   ❏

14. Mix the clear coat. Load this mixture into the paint gun. Spray two coats of clear over the entire panel. Allow the proper flash time between coats.   ❏

15. Label the back of the panel with the number of base and pearl coats. Cut the panel into nine squares, using the tape lines as a guide.   ❏

16. Hold the panels to the car to determine which combination matches the best.   ❏

Job Sheet 20-2

Name_____ Date _____ Instructor Review _____

Tri-Coat Finish

Objective

After completing this lab, the student should be able to spray a panel with tri-coat.

Equipment

Base color
Pearl coat
Clear coat
Spray gun
Hood
Wax and grease remover
320 or 400 grit sandpaper
Epoxy primer or urethane sealer

Safety Equipment

Safety glasses
Supplied air respirator
Impervious gloves
Paint suit

Procedure

Task Completed

1. Wash the hood with soap and water. De-wax. ❑

2. Sand the hood with 400 grit paper by hand or with 320 grit paper on a dual-action sander. Remove the sanding sludge. Blow it off and tack. ❑

3. Spray on a coat of epoxy primer or urethane sealer. Allow the proper time to dry. ❑

4. Mix the base coat to specifications. Load into the spray gun. ❑

5. Spray three coats of base. Allow the proper flash time between coats. Clean out the gun. ❑

6. Mix pearl or mid-coat. Load it into gun. Tack off the base coat. ❑

7. Spray two or three coats of pearl. Paint the first coat in the normal manner. The second coat should be sprayed at an angle to the first. This will minimize mottling. ❑

8. Check the pearl coat for signs of mottling. If any exist, spray a third coat, again at an angle to the second coat. Allow proper flash time between coats. Clean the gun. ❑

9. Mix the clear coat. Spray on two coats, using the proper flash time. Allow suitable dry time. ❑

10. Buff out any dirt or excessive "orange peel." ❑

Job Sheet 20-3

Name _____ Date _____ Instructor Review _____

Tri-Coat Spot Repairs

Objective

After completing this lab, the student should be able to make repairs on a tri-coat.

Equipment

Tri-coat refinished panel
Base coat
Pearl coat
Clear coat
Self-etching primer
600 wet paper
Spray gun
220, 320, 400 and 1000 grit paper
Sanding block
Wax and grease remover
Urethane primer

Safety Equipment

Safety glasses
Supplied air respirator
Impervious gloves
Paint suit

Procedure

Task Completed

1. Make a four-inch scratch in the middle of the refinished tri-coat hood. Clean the part with wax and grease remover. ❑

2. Repair the scratch by block sanding with 220 grit paper followed by 400 grit paper for featheredging. Remove sanding sludge and tack. ❑

3. Spray on self-etching primer and three coats of urethane primer. Guide coat the primer. Allow adequate dry time. ❑

4. Block sand the urethane primer with 320 dry paper on a hard block. Finish with 600 wet paper. Remove all traces of guide coat. ❑

5. Sand the rest of the hood with 1000 grit paper. ❑

6. Mix up the base coat as per label directions. Apply one coat to cover the primer only. The next coat should go out one inch further than the first coat. The third coat should be one inch further out from the second coat. Clean your gun and allow adequate flash time. ❑

7. Mix the pearl coat as per label directions. Tack off the hood. Spray the first coat of pearl to cover the base only. Spray the second coat at an angle to the first coat, finish about one inch from the edge of the first pearl coat. ❑

8. Check for mottling. If any exists, spray on a third coat. Hold the paint gun further away from the panel and spray at an angle to the second coat. Allow proper flash time. ❑

9. Mix the clear coat as per label directions and spray two coats over the entire hood. Allow sufficient time to dry. ❑

10. Sand and buff the hood. Check for a color match by viewing the hood from different angles. ❑

Job Sheet 20-4

Name_____ Date _____ Instructor Review _____

Color Wheel

Objective

After completing this lab, the student should have an understanding of the color wheel.

Equipment

Pure blue, red and yellow colors
White paper
Mixing vials

Safety Equipment

Safety glasses

Procedure

	Task Completed

1. Construct the color wheel by placing one inch drops of paint on a sheet of white paper. Mix one part yellow with one part blue to make green. ❏

2. The color wheel will be arranged like numbers on a clock. Place a drop of red at 12 o'clock, blue at 3 o'clock, green at 6 o'clock, and yellow at 9 o'clock. ❏

3. Mix one part red with one part blue. Place the resulting color between clock numbers one and two on the color wheel. Mix one part blue and one part green. Place this new color between clock numbers four and five. Mix one part yellow and one part green and place it between clock number seven and eight. Mix one part yellow with one part red. Position the resulting color between clock numbers ten and eleven. ❏

4. Mix two parts red and one part blue. Place it at clock number one. Then mix one part red with two parts blue and place it at clock number two. Next, mix two parts blue with one part green. Place the new color at clock number four. Mix one part blue with two parts green, placing it at clock number five. ❏

5. Now for the other side of the color wheel. Mix two parts of green with one part yellow. Place the resulting color at clock number seven. Then mix one part green with two parts yellow, placing it at clock number eight. For the following mix, blend two parts yellow with one part red, and position it at clock number ten. Finally, mix one part yellow with two parts red and place it at clock number eleven. ❏

6. Mix the color at clock number eleven with the color at clock number five. What is the result? _____ ❏

   _____

7. Mix the color between clock numbers seven and eight with blue. What is the result? _____ ❏

   _____

8. Mix the color at clock number eight with green. What is the result? _____ ❏

   _____

9. Mix the color at clock number two with yellow. What is the result?_____   ❑

10. Mix the color at clock number five with blue. What is the result? _____   ❑

Job Sheet 20-5

Name_____ Date _____ Instructor Review _____

Gun Adjustments

Objective

After completing this lab, the student should learn how gun adjustments can change color.

Equipment

Five pieces of 2' x 2' sheet metal
Wax/grease remover
Self etching primer
Silver or gold metallic single stage
   enamel paint
Spray gun
400 grit paper

Safety Equipment

Safety glasses
Paint respirator
Impervious gloves
Paint suit

Procedure

Task Completed

1. Cut out five pieces of 2' x 2' sheet metal. Measure carefully. The panels should be flat. Remove any arch by hammering. ❑

2. Clean the sheets with a wax and grease remover. Scuff sand with 400 grit paper. Blow off and tack. Spray on two coats of self etching primer. ❑

3. For this demonstration to work, you need to use a consistent spray technique. Mix the paint as per label directions and load it into the gun. Set up the spray gun by adjusting the fan and setting the air pressure and the fluid. ❑

4. Label the backside of the panels as follows: ❑

   1. Normal

   2. 10 lbs. less air pressure

   3. 10 lbs. more air pressure

   4. One turn more fluid

   5. One turn less fluid

5. Spray the piece labeled "normal." Set this panel aside. ❑

6. Adjust the gun to 10 lbs. less air pressure. Obtain the proper panel. Spray this panel, remembering to use a consistent technique. Set this panel aside. ❑

7. Adjust the gun to 10 lbs. more than the normal air pressure. Obtain the appropriate panel and spray. ❑

8. Set the gun to the normal air pressure. Turn the fluid control knob in one turn. Obtain the proper panel and spray. ❑

9. Turn the fluid control knob back to normal and then turn it out one turn. Obtain the proper panel and spray. ❑

10. After an adequate drying time, compare the modified panels to the normal panel.   ❑
     Fill out this chart:

	Spray **Drier or** **Wetter**	**Color** **Lighter or** **Darker**
10 lbs. less	_____	_____
10 lbs. more	_____	_____
1 turn in	_____	_____
1 turn out	_____	_____

Job Sheet 20-6

Name_____ Date _____ Instructor Review _____

Custom Painting Flames

Objective

After completing this lab, the student should have experience in one type of custom painting.

Equipment

Hood
400, 600, 1000 grit paper
Masking paper
Respirator
Sealer
Wax and grease remover
Three paint guns
Black, red, orange, and yellow basecoat

Safety Equipment

Safety glasses
Supplied air respirator
Impervious gloves
Paint suit

Task Completed

Procedure

1. Clean off the hood with a wax and grease remover. ❑

2. Sand with 400 grit paper by hand or 320 grit paper on a dual-action sander. Remove sanding sludge. Blow it off and tack. ❑

3. Spray one coat of sealer or epoxy primer on the hood. Allow it to dry. Nib sand as needed. ❑

4. Spray on three coats of black base coat. Allow proper flash time between coats. Spray on one coat of clear. Allow to dry overnight. ❑

5. Use fine line $1/8$" masking tape to lay out a flame design. Mask off areas to remain black with paper and tape. Sand areas to be painted with 600 grit paper. Be sure to sand at the edges of the tape. Sand through the clear coat. ❑

6. Load the red, orange and yellow base coat into separate paint guns. ❑

7. The idea is to spray the colors at the same time so the edges melt together. Spray yellow base on the front one third of the design. Immediately spray orange on the next third. Then spray the red on the last third. ❑

8. Spray other coats as needed in the same manner. When the black is totally covered, you can stop. Spray one coat of clear over the three colors. ❑

9. Remove the tape as soon as the clear coat is dust free. Allow to dry overnight. ❑

10. Wet sand all clear coat with 1000 grit paper. This sanding is intended to remove the tape edge. Remove all "orange peel." Do not sand into the base color. Spray two coats of clear over the entire hood. ❑

Review Questions

Name _____ Date _____ Instructor Review _____

1. The primary colors are _____,

   _____, _____,

   and _____.

2. The three dimensions of color are

   _____, _____,

   _____.

3. Technician A states that blue can be redder or yellower. Technician B believes that red can be bluer or yellower. Who is correct?

   A. Technician A
   B. Technician B
   C. Both A and B
   D. Neither A nor B

4. Metamerism results from different light sources.

   A. True
   B. False

5. Technician A adds white to increase the value. Technician B adds black to decrease the value. Who is correct?

   A. Technician A
   B. Technician B
   C. Both A and B
   D. Neither A nor B

6. When testing a color, Technician A adds tints as needed to change the color. Technician B adds tints only from the formula. Who is correct?

   A. Technician A
   B. Technician B
   C. Both A and B
   D. Neither A nor B

7. A slower drying solvent will make a metallic color darker.

   A. True
   B. False

8. When checking a metallic color for match, Technician A looks at the color head on. Technician B looks at the color from the side. Who is c orrect?

   A. Technician A
   B. Technician B
   C. Both A and B
   D. Neither A nor B

9. All of the following will make a metallic color darker except:

   A. Open fluid valve
   B. Decrease gun distance
   C. Increase fan width
   D. Slow down stroke

10. Flip flop can be corrected by adding white tint.

    A. True
    B. False

Chapter 21

Paint Problems and Final Detailing

Shop Assignment 21-1

Name_____ Date _____ Instructor Review _____

"As You Paint" Problems

You must correct these problems while you are in the booth and in less than fifteen minutes. Explain in a paragraph on how to solve each problem.

1. Dirt in the base coat

_____
_____
_____

2. Dirt in the clear coat

_____
_____
_____

3. "Fish Eyes"

_____
_____
_____

4. Lifting

_____
_____
_____

5. Sand scratch swelling

_____
_____
_____

6. Mottling

_____
_____
_____

7. Air hose dragged over wet paint

_____

_____

_____

8. Tack rag gouges wet paint

_____

_____

_____

9. Paint suit touches wet paint

_____

_____

_____

10. Runs

_____

_____

_____

Shop Assignment 21-2

Name_____ Date _____ Instructor Review _____

"What Is the Problem?"

1.

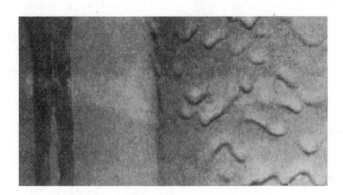

Name of problem:_____

How can you fix this? _____

_____

_____

_____

2.

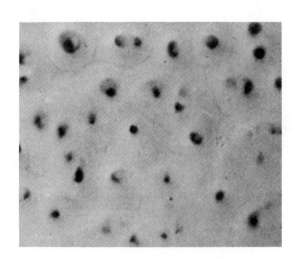

Name of problem:_____

How can you fix this? _____

_____

_____

_____

3.

Name of problem:_____

How can you fix this? _____

_____

_____

_____

4.

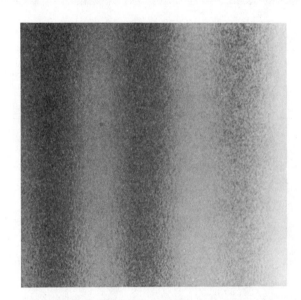

Name of problem:_____

How can you fix this? _____

_____

_____

_____

5.

Name of problem:_____

How can you fix this? _____

_____

_____

_____

6.

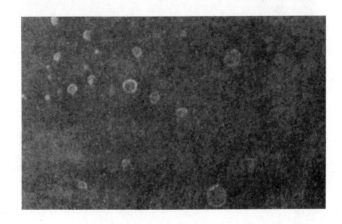

Name of problem:_____

How can you fix this? _____

_____

_____

_____

7.

Name of problem:_____

How can you fix this? _____

_____

_____

_____

8.

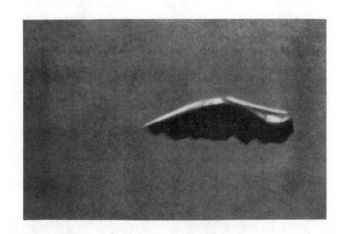

Name of problem:_____

How can you fix this? _____

_____

_____

_____

9.

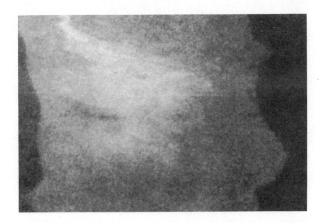

Name of problem:_____

How can you fix this? _____

_____

_____

_____

Job Sheet 21-1

Name_____ Date _____ Instructor Review _____

Sand and Buff Fresh Urethane Paint

Objective

After completing this lab, the student should be able to color sand and buff out dirt and minor "orange peel" from a fresh urethane BC/CC paint job.

Equipment

Buffer
Fresh 12–24 hrs BC/CC Panel
Water hose or squeeze bottle
Pad cleaning tool
1500 grit paper
Ruler, cut into 1" sections
Sanding pad
Squeegee
Hand glaze

Safety Equipment

Safety glasses

Procedure

Task Completed

1. Examine the paint surface. Note the location of the dirt and excessive "orange peel." ❑

2. On dirt, allow 1500 grit sandpaper to soak in water for fifteen minutes. Then cut and wrap the paper around a one inch piece of ruler or other thin, flat piece of wood. Sand on the dirt spot with a circular motion. Try not to sand on the adjacent paint. Sand until the dirt is level with the surrounding paint. ❑

3. On excessive "orange peel," again soak 1500 grit paper in water for fifteen minutes. Then wrap the paper around a sanding pad. Sand "orange peel" with a small circular motion. Avoid long, straight strokes. Use a water hose or squeeze bottle to float away sanded particles. Use a rubber squeegee to check your work. When the sanded surfaces are uniformly dull with no shiny dots, you are finished. ❑

4. Remove the water and sanding sludge from the panel. ❑

5. Your instructor will demonstrate proper technique. Clean the buffer pad with a tool. Apply a six inch ribbon of fine finishing compound to the paint surface. Working in one small area at a time, move the buffer back and forth. If the buffer speed is adjustable, use about 1000 rpm. ❑

6. Be very careful around edges and body lines. The buffer will grab onto these areas and rub the paint off before you know it. Also do not apply excessive pressure to the buffer. ❑

7. Sanded areas should brighten after buffing. You will need to buff until you remove all scratches and the surface is glossy. ❑

Task Completed

8. Carefully inspect the surface for sand scratches. If you find them, continue buffing. You will notice that buffing removes some of the original gloss present in the clear coat.   ❏

9. When all of the scratches have been removed, apply a ribbon of hand glaze.   ❏

10. Work the hand glaze into the clear coat and wipe off with a soft cloth.   ❏

Job Sheet 21-2

Name_____ Date _____ Instructor Review _____

Buff Faded Single-Stage Paint

Objective

After completing this lab, the student should be able to buff a faded single-stage paint job.

Equipment

Buffer
Pad cleaning tool
Rubbing compound
Paint brush
Hand glaze

Safety Equipment

Safety glasses

Procedure

Task Completed

1. Examine the paint. Usually the upper surfaces fade the most. The faded upper surfaces will need the most buffing. The sides, where the paint has not been exposed to direct sun, may need very little buffing. ❑

2. Wash the car to remove any particles that could scratch the paint. ❑

3. Buff a two feet by two feet area at one time. Start on the roof. Use a paint brush to distribute the compound over the designated area. ❑

4. Your instructor will demonstrate proper technique. Keep the electrical cord over your shoulder and out of the way as you buff. Hold the pad at a slight angle to the surface. Apply pressure and work back and forth in the two feet by two feet area. ❑

5. Be careful around the body lines and panel edges. If you buff on an edge, it will immediately burn through to the primer. ❑

6. You can apply pressure as long as you have the compound between the pad and the paint. When the compound is used up, do not bear down on the buffer. You can burn the paint that way. ❑

7. When you have finished with the first area, move on the roof and continue buffing. Continue until you have buffed the entire car. Clean the pad when it becomes clogged with paint. ❑

8. Do not buff any longer than it takes to get the shine back. There is a finite amount of paint on the car. The more you buff off, the less paint there is. ❑

9. When you have finished buffing the entire car, you can apply a hand glaze. The glaze will remove most of the swirl marks caused by the buffing. Spread a small amount of glaze on the surface. Work it in with a circular motion. Remove the haze with a soft cloth. ❑

10. Clean the compound out of the openings and off of the glass. ❑

Job Sheet 21-3

Name_____ Date _____ Instructor Review _____

"Fisheyes"

Objective

After completing this lab, the student should be able to recognize and correct a "fisheye" problem.

Equipment

Fender gun
Base coat
400 and 600 grit paper
Epoxy primer
Wax/Grease remover
Wax and grease remover
Silicon spray
Rag

Safety Equipment

Safety glasses
Paint respirator
Impervious gloves
Paint suit

Procedure

Task Completed

1. Wash the fender with soap and water. Clean with a wax and grease remover. ❑

2. Scuff sand the fender with 400 grit paper or use 320 grit paper on a DA. Blow off and tack. ❑

3. Mix epoxy primer as per label directions and spray on a coat of it. Allow it to dry. ❑

4. Apply a small amount of silicon spray to a rag. Wipe the treated rag over the fender. ❑

5. Mix the base coat as per label direction. Load into the paint gun. Spray the fender. Describe (in the space below) what the paint looks like. _____ ❑

_____

_____

_____

6. Use a heat lamp or infrared lamp dryer to rapidly dry the panel. ❑

7. Clean the panel with a wax and grease remover. Wet sand with 600 grit paper. Be careful not to dig into the fresh paint. Sand out the craters. ❑

8. Clean the panel with a wax and grease remover. Blow off and tack. ❑

9. Spray on another coat of base. If the "fisheyes" reappear, repeat the cleaning, sanding, and cleaning process. ❑

Job Sheet 21-4

Name_____ Date _____ Instructor Review _____

Lifting

Objective

After completing this lab, the student should be able to recognize and correct lifting.

Equipment

Fender
Wax/grease remover
Lacquer primer
Lacquer top coat
400, 600, and 1,000 grit sandpaper
Water based primer

Safety Equipment

Safety glasses
Supplied air respirator
Impervious gloves
Paint suit

Procedure

Task Completed

1. Lifting is a problem resulting from an incompatibility in the refinish materials. This can be from sandwiching lacquer and enamel. It can also be caused by painting over a previously refinished surface. ❑

2. Wash the fender with soap and water. Clean with a wax and grease remover. Sand with 400 grit paper, and then remove the sanding sludge. Blow off and tack. ❑

3. Mix the lacquer primer. Load this mixture into the paint gun and spray three coats. Mix the lacquer top coat and spray four coats. Allow it to dry overnight. ❑

4. Make a six-inch scratch on the fender. Repair the scratch by block sanding with 400 grit paper. Featheredge at least one inch of each layer: Lacquer top coat, lacquer primer and the original finish. Spray the bare metal with self etching primer. Then spray on two coats of urethane primer. Next spray on a guide coat and allow it to dry. ❑

5. Block sand the primer and fender with 600 grit paper and water. Remove all of the guide coat and sanding sludge. Blow off and tack. ❑

6. Mix a urethane base coat. Spray on one wet coat. There should be lifting where the lacquer paint was sanded through. ❑

7. Position a heat lamp to rapidly dry the paint. After five minutes, use 1000 grit paper and water to smooth the deep scratches. Do not sand too deep and roll up the paint. Spray a dry coat over the scratches. The purpose is to build up a dry barrier so the solvent will not penetrate. Apply three more dry coats. Allow proper flash time and tack off the overspray in between the coats. ❑

8. Spray on a medium wet coat of paint. If lifting continues, put the heat lamp on the lifted area for ten minutes. ❑

9. To correct the lifting problem, sand the entire fender with 600 grit paper. Clean, blow off and tack. Spray on one coat of a water-based primer. ❑

10. Allow the water-based primer to dry, usually twenty-four hours. Sand to remove "orange peel" and spray base coat. ❑

Review Questions

Name_____ Date _____ Instructor Review _____

1. The original finish seeping through the new top coat color is called _____.

2. Technician A states that solvent pop is caused by insufficient flash time. Technician B believes the solvent pop is caused by improper use of an HVLP paint gun. Who is correct?

   A. Technician A
   B. Technician B
   C. Both A and B
   D. Neither A nor B

3. Painting lacquer over fresh, air dried enamel will cause lifting.

   A. True
   B. False

4. "Fish eyes" are caused by _____ _____.

5. Burn through when buffing is most likely to happen on the edges of panels.

   A. True
   B. False

6. Before buffing a newly painted urethane clear coat, Technician A uses 1000 grit paper. Technician B uses 1500 grit paper. Who is correct?

   A. Technician A
   B. Technician B
   C. Both A and B
   D. Neither A nor B

7. A decal can be removed with a _____ _____.

8. To remove overspray on a windshield, Technician A uses a razor blade. Technician B uses a rag dipped in thinner. Who is correct?

   A. Technician A
   B. Technician B
   C. Both A and B
   D. Neither A nor B

9. Technician A buffs urethane clear within 24 hours of painting. Technician B buffs the urethane clear after 36 hours of painting. Who is correct?

   A. Technician A
   B. Technician B
   C. Both A and B
   D. Neither A nor B

10. The buffer should always be moving.

    A. True
    B. False

Chapter 22

Repair Cost Estimating and Entrepreneurship

Job Sheet 22-1

Name_____ Date _____ Instructor Review _____

Single Panel Repair Estimate

Objective

After completing this lab, the student should be able to write an estimate of vehicle repair.

Equipment

Vehicle with repairable dent
Collision estimate guide
Calculator
Estimate sheets

Safety Equipment

Safety glasses

Procedure

	Task Completed
1. Walk around the vehicle and take note of all the damage.	❏
2. Fill out the estimate sheet with the customer's name, address, and phone number. Write down the vehicle year, make, model, VIN, and paint code.	❏
3. Carefully examine the dented panel. For buckled dents, use your hand to measure the size of the damage. Figure two hours for each hand that can fit in the damage. Add an hour for gaining access to the back side of the panel.	❏
4. If the damage is door dings or hail dents, figure an hour for each dent.	❏
5. Make a check mark in the repair column and write "Repair _____."	❏
6. Look at the estimating guide "P" pages. Read what is included and not included on the panel you are working on.	❏
7. Find the type of vehicle you are working on in the guide. Turn to the page listing the panel you are repairing. At the top of that part section is a time for refinishing the panel. Write that number in the paint labor column.	❏
8. Figure paint blend time. Go to the "P" pages for paint blend. You should blend the panels on either side of the repair panel. Make a separate line stating "blend paint" and put the hours under paint labor.	❏

9. If the paint is base coat/clear coat, go to the "P" pages for clear time. You should write a line stating "clear coat" and put the hours under paint labor.

❑

10. Total up the body labor and paint labor. Multiply each by the labor ratio to get a dollar figure. Enter these on the appropriate lines. Take the paint labor hours times the material cost per paint hour. Put this dollar figure on the line for parts. Multiply the parts by the tax ratio. Enter this figure on the tax line. Add the lines together for the estimate total.

❑

Job Sheet 22-2

Name_____ Date _____ Instructor Review _____

Single Panel Replacement Estimate

Objective

After completing this lab, the student should be able to write an estimate for the replacement of a single panel.

Equipment

Damaged vehicle
Estimating guides
Calculator
Estimate sheets

Safety Equipment

Safety glasses

Procedure

Task Completed

1. Walk around the vehicle and take note of all of the damage. ☐

2. Fill out the estimate sheet with the customer's name, address, and phone number. Write down the vehicle year, model, make, VIN and paint code. ☐

3. Examine the part that is to be replaced. Are any fasteners damaged? Will anything else need to be taken off to get this part removed? ☐

4. Look at the "P" pages in the estimating guide. Read over what is covered and not covered in replacing this part. Will the part need to be rustproofed? ☐

5. Find the type of vehicle you are working on in the guide. Turn to the section listing the panel you are replacing. ☐

6. Put a check mark in the replace column. Write "replace _____" on the line. Put the price of the part in the parts column. ☐

7. Look up the replacement labor time. Enter this number in the body labor column. ☐

8. Find the refinish time for the part. Add any edging time. Put this total in the paint labor column. ☐

9. Figure blend and clear coat time as before. ☐

10. If the part needs to be rustproofed, make another line "rustproof part" with the price of the rustproof material in the parts column. Put the time it takes to mix, apply and clean up in the body labor column. ☐

11. Total and multiply as before. ☐

Job Sheet 22-3

Name_____ Date _____ Instructor Review _____

Estimate

Objective

After completing this lab, the student should be able to write an estimate.

Equipment

Damaged vehicle
Estimating guide
Calculator
Estimate sheets

Safety Equipment

Safety glasses

Procedure

Task Completed

1. Walk around the vehicle and note all of the damage. ❑

2. Fill out the estimate sheet with the customer's name, address and phone number. Write down the vehicle year, make, model, VIN and paint code. ❑

3. Read the "P" pages for all damaged sections of the car. ❑

4. Start at the front and work towards the back. Use the estimating guide as a map. Check over each section to make sure you did not miss any parts. ❑

5. Estimate frame damage labor time using this rationale:

   Set up on machine and hang gauges   3 hours
   Each damaged condition per rail   2 hours

   For example, if the car has sidesway on both rails and sag on the rail, then it would be three hours for set up time, plus four hours for the sidesway and two hours for the sag. This would bring the total to nine hours. ❑

6. Read the "P" pages about the overlap time for body and paint labor. ❑

7. If the moldings are to be reused, figure on half an hour to remove, clean, tape and install. ❑

8. Figure panel repair, replacement, refinish, edging, blend, clear coat and rustproofing time as before. ❑

9. Total and multiply as before. ❑

Review Questions

Name_____ Date _____ Instructor Review _____

1. Who has the final approval of vehicle repairs?

   A. Vehicle owner
   B. Insurance company

2. Technician A uses collision estimating guides for appropriate under hood dimensions. Technician B uses collision estimating guides for labor times. Who is correct?

   A. Technician A
   B. Technician B
   C. Both A and B
   D. Neither A nor B

3. R and I means to _____ and

   _____.

4. The computer brain is called _____.

5. Technician A states that the rear bumper removal is included in replacing a quarter panel. Technician B believes that refinish time is included in replacing the quarter panel. Who is correct?

   A. Technician A
   B. Technician B
   C. Both A and B
   D. Neither A nor B

6. Estimates are good for ninety days.

   A. True
   B. False

7. A vehicle is _____ if the repair cost exceeds the value of the vehicle.

8. Overlap needs to be subtracted from the labor time when two adjacent panels are replaced.

   A. True
   B. False

9. Ten minutes is 0.3 hr.

   A. True
   B. False

10. Direct repair programs are very beneficial to small body shops.

    A. True
    B. False